9

SIMPLE FOOD

SIMPLE FOOD
LIZ & GERD SEEBER

DORLING KINDERSLEY · LONDON

A Jill Norman Book

First published in Great Britain in 1987
by Dorling Kindersley Limited,
9 Henrietta Street, London WC2E 8PS

British Library Cataloguing in Publication Data
Seeber, Gerd Christian
Simple food.
1. Cookery
I. Title   II. Seeber, Liz
641.5′55   TX652

ISBN 0-86318-203-8
ISBN 0-86318-204-6 Pbk

Jacket photograph of authors by Jessica Strang

Computerset by MFK Typesetting Ltd, Hitchin, Hertfordshire
Printed in Great Britain by Butler and Tanner, Frome, Somerset

CONTENTS

CONTENTS

CONTENTS

CONTENTS

CONTENTS

SPRING

ASPARAGUS GALORE

Once a year invite your friends to share this short-lived indigenous delicacy with you to the full. You'll need nothing special in terms of equipment – a big saucepan or two, and some kitchen string.

Asparagus – hot and cold

English goat cheeses

Strawberry sorbet

Biddenden Ortega 1985
Chinon or Bourgeuil

SHOPPING LIST

ASPARAGUS – if at all possible buy it only the day before the meal if not on the day itself, though do order in advance if your requirements run to several pounds. Watch out for freshness; the cut ends tell if the sticks were harvested recently, or too much moisture has been lost – they look wooden and fibrous when dry. Check that the tips are intact and closed like buds – they snap easily in transport and only too often a decapitated stalk hides at the centre of a bundle. Reject sticks that are limp or no longer round because they have been squeezed dry. It helps both for cooking and portioning out if they are approximately uniform in size and shape. Allow about two dozen sticks per person; indigenous asparagus is lighter than the white continental variety and has but a short season, so why not enjoy it to the full while it lasts? In any case, get a few extra sticks for testing when you cook them. At home rinse the bundles under a gentle stream of cold water to remove sand and earth from the cut ends, wrap each in a clean damp cloth, and store in your refrigerator unless you intend cooking them soon.

LEMONS – for acidulating the asparagus water, half a lemon per pan; plus one quarter of a big lemon per guest to dress the asparagus cold, and an additional quarter each if you want to offer finger bowls at the end. Slightly under-ripe lemons are a brighter greenish yellow than mature ones, giving a crisper accent to the eye.

BUTTER – for the hot asparagus. Don't spoil the flavour of fresh asparagus with some cold-storage product from the EEC butter mountain. Buy unsalted fresh butter from Cornwall or just slightly salted from Wales, for example. Assuming two dozen or so sticks per guest, and that half will be eaten hot, allow about 1 1/2 oz (40 g) each.

OLIVE OIL – for the cold asparagus, but if everyone pours their own – on average perhaps 1 fl oz (25 ml) per head – it's wise to err on the generous side. Olive oil has so many uses it doesn't matter if you have some left over. Buy a good oil – Tuscan *extra vergine*, for example, from the first cold pressing – but look around first. There are some silly prices being asked for pretty bottles rather than contents, while supermarkets have begun to import their own brands you might try.

ENGLISH GOAT CHEESES – Patrick Rance writes that goats are being more widely milked in Britain for cheesemaking than ever before (*The Great British Cheese Book*, Papermac, 1983). Indeed, even idigenous *pyramides* are to be found nowadays. Ask around if necessary, a shop like Neal's Yard or Harrods in London, with a good turnover of British cheese, is well worth locating also for future needs. Buy by taste and eye – it's difficult to state exactly how much in weight you should allow per head. A soft wedge of a fresh white cheese with a cool clean taste; plus a little of one dusted with charcoal and salt, or rolled in herbs; and one more, which might be harder and growing spicy with a little age – that's what we'd imagine on each plate. Store the cheeses in the larder or a cool room if possible, covering only the cut surfaces – cheeses tend to sweat and go soggy in the refrigerator, where they can't breathe.

STRAWBERRY SORBET – few puddings are prepared more easily than a strawberry sorbet. You will need 4 oz (125 g) of strawberries, the juice of a quarter orange, a few drops of lemon juice and 2 oz (50 g) of caster sugar for 1 generous helping. Alternatively, choose a proprietary brand, and store as directed on the packet.

OTHER INGREDIENTS – fresh bread, if you like, for serving with the asparagus and cheeses, white and a little granary; salt and freshly ground black pepper.

WINES – ortega is the name of an early ripening grape grown at Biddenden Vineyards in Kent, where it's made into a prize-winning medium white, with a strong flowery nose and plenty of fruit to follow. You could serve it as an aperitif, and then with the asparagus – unfortunately no easy companion for any wine. Contemplate changing to red as you reach the salad stage of the asparagus. Chinon and Bourgueil, also St Nicholas de Bourgueil, are uncomplicated wines from these three villages in the Loire valley. Made from the cabernet franc grape, they are best when young and slightly chilled, which makes them suitable to be drunk before meals too. Once found, they should not be expensive. Like the ortega, we find them very drinkable – for a real feast it would be unwise to allow less than half a bottle of each, white and red, per head.

PREPARATION AND PRECOOKING

To make your own strawberry sorbet, on the night or in the morning before the party, gently rinse the strawberries in cold water, let drip and spread over a double layer of kitchen paper – the less water that remains, the more concentrated your sorbet will taste. With a small pointed knife cut around the stems and leaves. Try to pull them with the hard hulls from the core of each berry, but don't worry if you don't always succeed. Put all the sorbet ingredients – quantities as given in the shopping list or in proportion – into a bowl, mix gently, and let stand at room temperature for 2 hours or so. When the time is up, process or liquidize the mix, or push it through a sieve if you don't have a machine, and pour it into a container suitable for freezing. Place the container in your freezer or the ice compartment of a refrigerator. Stir, around the edges and corners especially, after 1 hour or so and once or twice again, to break up big ice crystals. For an ice cream maker, follow the manufacturer's instructions.

Perhaps 2 hours before you want to get ready for your guests, see that the wine is getting cool, and transfer the sorbet, if you made it yourself, from the freezer to the refrigerator; if you bought it, follow the manufacturer's instructions.

Choose a saucepan big enough in diameter to take the asparagus lying down, and fill it with water so that the sticks will be well covered when you put them in – later, not now. Add salt, 1 heaped tablespoon per gallon (4.5 litres), and place over a high heat, lid on. Do this early on, for even with a high heat it can take as long as 20 minutes to bring a gallon of water to the boil.

Put the asparagus – each bundle or bunch of sticks approximately similar in length – on a cutting board. With a big sharp knife chop about 1 inch (2.5 cm) or so off the dry bottom ends. Discard the ends, untie the bundles, and rinse the individual sticks in cold water if they are still sandy, but be careful not to damage the tips. Don't bother about peeling – when eating by hand, dunking the sticks in melted butter or olive oil and lemon juice, the extra stiffness of the hard outer skin is quite welcome. Drain, rebundle and tie with kitchen string, but leave loose the few extra sticks, of average thickness, you bought for testing. Now divide the asparagus – one half to be eaten cold, which you can cook right now; the other hot, to be cooked later.

When the water is boiling fast, add the juice of half a lemon – this helps to preserve the green of the asparagus. Holding them by the string, carefully lower the bundles to the bottom, adding two or three of the loose sticks. Let the water come back to the boil and reduce the heat so that it moves only gently, or it will damage the tips. Keep the lid off – steam trapped under it has a higher temperature than boiling water, and turns vegetables grey. Set the timer and test after 10 minutes – lift out a stick, let it cool for a moment and bite the tip, middle, and bottom – 12-14 minutes should be enough for all but the thickest stalks to soften to the point when they offer no more than a pleasant resistance to the bite. When they are done, switch off the heat, lift the bundles out by their strings, cut open, and spread on a double layer of kitchen paper to absorb surplus moisture. Let the sticks cool, but put the lid back on the water – it'll stay hot for quite some time, when you can use it again for the hot asparagus.

Weigh out the butter for the hot asparagus – say 1 ½ oz (40 g) per 12 sticks – and put in a small saucepan, ready for melting when the hot asparagus is about to be served. Find a sauce boat or jug to offer it in.

Rinse the lemons you'll need for the cold dressing. Cut them up – a quarter wedge per head – arrange on a suitable dish, and set aside in a cool place. Measure out enough of the olive oil into a jug or bottle suitable for passing around, and arrange the cold asparagus sticks on a platter, decorated with extra lemon wedges if you like.

Last in this preparatory stage, if your cheeses are in the refrigerator, take them out now – they won't have any taste if they are too cold. Arrange them on a platter, flat basket or board decked out with some big green leaves – plane, chestnut, vine or ivy, for example.

COOKING AND PRESENTATION

You know by now how to cook asparagus, and how long it takes, so all you need do is a repeat. Have the water standing by – i.e. ready to boil again, topped up from the kettle if necessary – so that you can begin as soon as everyone has a glass of wine, and appetites are sharpening. You could of course turn the sequence round, and serve cold before hot – it's up to you.

While the asparagus is cooking, melt the butter over moderate heat; scoop off and discard the surface froth if you like (these so-called impurities sometimes removed by clarifying are perfectly edible) but, rather more important, don't burn the butter – it should be golden, not brown, when it comes to table. Warm the sauce boat or whatever vessel you'll offer it in with hot water.

Let the hot sticks dry for a moment as before, but then work quickly – arrange them on a platter, or individual plates, and serve without delay. Offer the butter, salt, fresh black pepper and a little bread to mop up with on the side.

If you like, change wines after this course.

Offer the cold asparagus. The idea is simple, one we picked up in Tuscany – pour a little oil over the tips, sprinkle them with lemon juice, salt and pepper, and you have a most delicious hand salad. You could present the cheeses now too – that way variety is increased, and your work as host reduced. Only the sorbet remains to be served.

FOR SPECIAL OCCASIONS

Good ingredients can go far and work out
rather more cheaply per head than is often
thought. You'll need only one piece of
equipment a little out of the ordinary for this
recipe – a fish kettle of the wide variety,
sometimes called a turbotière; alternatively try
a big roasting pan with a double layer of
perforated foil on the bottom so that you can
lift the fish out, with more foil to make a lid.

Parma ham with melon

Poached turbot; new potatoes; sauce hollandaise

*Small salad of lamb's lettuce, sorrel and rocket,
with walnut oil and lemon dressing*

Brie

*White wines made from the classic chardonnay
grape, comparing Australian, Californian and
others if there are enough drinkers*

SHOPPING LIST

TURBOT – to us the best of flat if not all fish, with firm white flesh,
at times half the price of salmon. Grown specimens may reach 45
lb (20 kg) in weight, but chicken turbots can be small enough for

just 2 portions. Calculate at least 8 oz (250 g) per person, and ask your fishmonger a few days in advance what the chances are of finding a smallish turbot in the market; brill is a good alternative. Order so that the fishmonger himself receives the turbot only on the day you intend cooking it, and make a note of the weight when collecting the fish. At home unwrap it at once, remove absorbent paper that may stick to the skin, cover loosely with foil and store in the refrigerator.

PARMA HAM – prosciutto di Parma – cured by a process of salting and drying in air, so avoid the end cuts, which are better suited to cooking. A little further in, the meat should be free of crusty white salt marks, which would be a sign that it has not been cut for some time, and of an even, brownish pink, with rather more lean than fat. The fat should be white and firm. Unlike some of the lesser varieties of raw ham, Parma ham needs to be cut by machine as thinly as possible to do justice to its flavour and delicate texture. It's a pleasure to watch an expert lay out slice after slice, with paper between the layers that would otherwise stick and tear on separation. Seeing the slices come off the machine, you can easily judge the size of a portion by eye – 2-3 slices, less than 2 oz (50 g) per starter. Try not to put anything on top of the ham in your shopping basket; provided it is wrapped well, it will keep moist enough for a day or even two in the refrigerator.

MELON – honeydew is the kind usually served to counter the saltiness of Parma ham, but it can be a little elusive as it ripens only slowly. No sweet melon is ready to be eaten unless it gives off a pleasant scent, and colour is an indicator – look for a deep yellow rather than green rind. Choose a canteloupe or gallia melon if they are more likely to be ripe, or more suitable in size – you need 1 good wedge per portion with the ham, no more. Rinse, wipe dry and store in the refrigerator if your purchase is ripe; leave it out if you are not sure. Alternatively, Parma ham is perfectly good enough to be eaten on its own, with a little black pepper; or, as Elizabeth David suggests in her classic *Italian Food* (Penguin, 1987), even more delicious with small pieces of fresh unsalted butter, though without bread.

NEW POTATOES – Jerseys are often praised above all others, but tend to be expensive. To our tastes, Italian or Spanish new potatoes can be just as sweet, at a fraction of the price. Choose small ones, so that 4 or 5 amount to a good handful or single helping.

LAMB'S LETTUCE, SORREL AND ROCKET – in spring the last two can be found wild if you know what you are looking for, but substitute watercress if necessary. Make the lamb's lettuce your base, say three quarters of the total salad, using the others for acidity and spice. Avoid wilting or over-grown leaves. Buy quantities by eye, remembering that, once dressed, little leaves will compact. Keep them in the salad tray of your refrigerator, making sure they are dry, don't get squashed, and get at least a breath of air.

LEMON – juice for the salad dressing, and just a sprinkle for the sauce hollandaise; 1 lemon for 6 helpings.

BUTTER – if you can't find a ripe melon and decide to follow Elizabeth David's advice, buy unsalted fresh butter to accompany the Parma ham, and use the same top quality to make the hollandaise – calculate 1 oz (25 g) per head for that, though, as with all butter-based sauces, you can use a little more if you wish.

EGGS – for the hollandaise count 2 yolks to make enough for up to 3 portions, 3 for up to 6 portions, 4 for up to 10; but, as with a mayonnaise, keep a couple extra in reserve just to ensure nothing will go wrong.

WALNUT OIL – for the salad dressing. Various makes are on the market – check it's from a recent pressing, or it may be rancid. Luckily walnut oil is sold in small containers, and a little will go far. It's well worth trying. Keep in the refrigerator.

BRIE – brie de Meaux, brie de Melun, and coulommiers are relations in descending order of standing, and not easily found in perfect condition, so start looking for them a little in advance –

different shops get their supplies at different times. Excellent coulommiers-type cheeses are also made in Britain nowadays, and you might profitably concentrate on them if you have problems with their French cousins. If you can't sniff and taste before you buy, at least look – brie de Meaux is whiter and milder than Melun, and comes in bigger and thinner wheels; if it's been cut already, it should bulge at the opened sides, displaying a uniform glistening core between upper and lower crust, but don't buy if the crusts are about to meet, with over-ripe insides having run out from between. Store the cheese in a cool place or refrigerator if necessary, covering the cut sides only.

WINES – chardonnay is the single grape responsible for Chablis, blanc de blancs Champagne, and those illustrious big white burgundies, Meursault and Montrachet for example. However, excellent wines, sold under the varietal name chardonnay, are made with it in Australia, California and South Tirol, to name but three places. Unlike many other whites, it matures well, so you might compare not only regions but also young with old. Here are some names to look for: 1984 Chardonnay, J Tiefenbrunner (South Tirol/Alto Adige, Italy); Sainsbury's Californian Pinot Chardonnay; Wyndham Estate 1984 Hunter Valley Chardonnay (Australia); 1981 Gold Seal Vineyards Chardonnay, New York State.

PREPARATION AND PRECOOKING

Some 2 hours before the appointed time, lift the drainer from the fish kettle, take the turbot from the refrigerator, gently rinse it under cold water and place it, dark side up, on the drainer so that it can warm a little. Make sure your wines are getting cold, and put the melon in the refrigerator if it isn't there already.

An hour or so later, wash the potatoes in cold water, until all earth has gone. Scrub with a hard brush, but leave the skins intact. Set aside to dry.

Sort the salad leaves. Remove roots, if any, from the lamb's lettuce, and over-long stems from the sorrel and rocket. Rinse the leaves in cold water. Lay them out to dry between layers of kitchen paper in a cool place.

Half fill the fish kettle with water. Our turbotière holds 2 gallons (9 litres) at a little under half mark, and takes some 24 minutes to come to the boil over a high heat, lid on. Count 7 minutes per pound (500 g) of weight to calculate how long it will take to cook your fish.

Prepare a bain-marie for the hollandaise. Choose a mixing bowl in which you can whisk the sauce – a few drops of water, yolks and melting butter – not much, in other words, but you will need room to beat a wire whisk in it. Find a roasting tin or flat saucepan big enough to let you set the mixing bowl inside, with a little hot water around its lower third, so that the ingredients in the bowl will get warmed only gently by avoiding direct contact with the heat.

Take the butter for the hollandaise from the refrigerator – 1 oz (25 g) per helping – cut it into smallish cubes and set aside, where it can warm a little but not melt. Separate the yolks from the egg whites – 2 to make up to 3 helpings of the sauce, 3 for up to 6, 4 for up to 10. Put the yolks in the mixing bowl of your bain-marie and set aside.

COOKING AND PRESENTATION

Add 2 heaped tablespoons of salt per gallon (4.5 litres) of water to the turbotière, put in the fish on the drainer, and set to boil, lid on.

Heat some lightly salted water for the potatoes, but don't put them in yet.

Take the melon from the refrigerator, cut it in half with a big sharp knife, discard the seeds, and portion as required. Trim off the rinds if you like. Arrange the wedges on a dish suitable for serving.

Unwrap the Parma ham. Lay out each portion on a flat plate, only just overlapping the slices.

Remove the lid from the turbotière as the water is beginning to roll, reduce the heat so that it barely shivers, and set the timer – 7 minutes per pound (500 g).

Drop the potatoes into fast boiling water, let it come back to the boil, then reduce to a lively simmer. Set the timer for 12 minutes.

Serve the first course, with fresh black pepper or cold butter if there is no melon; in any case, offer them as alternatives if you like.

Try a potato after 12 minutes – by bite rather than stabbing. Drain and keep hot in the dry saucepan, lid on.

Make the hollandaise. Pour hot but not scalding water from the tap or kettle into the bain-marie and place over low heat. Add 1 tablespoon of tepid water to the yolks, plus a good pinch of salt and pepper. Place the mixing bowl in the water bath, and whisk until smooth. Put in two of the butter cubes, whisking until they have melted completely. Continue this process, adding the cubes in fours or fives, dissolving them completely before you add more or the sauce will separate. Make sure the mixture gets enough but not too much heat as you continue to whisk. It will take a few minutes to make the sauce, and you should just be able to hold the top of the mixing bowl with your bare hand; if it gets too hot, lift the mixing bowl out of the bath for a moment, and reduce the heat. When the whisk leaves trails that close up only slowly, beat in a few drops of lemon juice and take the bowl from the bath.

Season with salt, pepper and a little more lemon juice if necessary, but be careful, especially with the last – to our taste at least, many recipes use far too much of it. Serve as soon as possible, in a sauce boat or jug preheated with hot water; if necessary leave the sauce in the warm, not hot, bain-marie – if it's well made, it will stay stable for a while.

If the sauce separates because you worked too fast, start over with a fresh bowl and yolk, whisking in the separated sauce more slowly. If the eggs scramble because you allowed the sauce to get too hot, no repair is possible. Start again. Alternatively, serve the turbot and new potatoes with cold butter only – they are good enough, maybe even more subtle, this way.

When the turbot is done, carefully lift the drainer from the kettle, slide the fish on to a platter and present at table. Slit and pull away the dark skin with a flat knife. Make an incision between the two fillets thus exposed, down to the backbone. Lift them out, whole or in sections per portion, straight on to plates. Pull away the little bones around the outsides and put them on a separate plate – there is just a little flesh on them, but they are fiddly to pick clean, so leave them for later. Remove the backbone, lifting it by the tail. Serve the two bottom fillets, leaving behind the white skin of the underside.

Dress the salad after you have finished the main course. First pour over a little of the walnut oil. Toss until all the leaves are bright and shiny. Next sprinkle on a little lemon juice, salt and fresh black pepper to taste, toss again, and serve with the brie.

COOL AND EASY

A light meal, with a minimum of preparation and cooking time, suitable also for a charcoal grill in the garden.

Iced cucumber salad, with yoghurt dressing

Paillard of veal from the grill

Mixed spring vegetables – artichokes, carrots, peas and spinach – stewed in their juices

Fruit flan from the pâtisserie counter

A young greenish wine – a grüner veltliner or riesling from the slopes of the Danube

SHOPPING LIST

CUCUMBER – a large cucumber will serve 4. It should be round, firm, without damaged skin. Wash it in cold water, dry, and refrigerate.

SPRING VEGETABLES – an artichoke, a few baby carrots, a couple of handfuls of peas in their pods, plus a similar quantity of spinach leaves per person. Young artichokes have small tight globes with upper stems that are edible, similar in texture to the hearts. Fresh carrots show strong colouring and rich foliage, and have a spicy scent. Pea pods ought to be moist, pale green, and snap rather than shrivel between your fingers.

LEMON – half a fruit to make yoghurt dressing for up to 4 portions; plus a quarter wedge for each paillard.

CHIVES – also for the yoghurt dressing; half an average bunch for 4 portions.

GARLIC – 1-2 cloves per 4 helpings when cooking the vegetables.

PAPRIKA – buy only a tiny container of the sweet Hungarian variety, as it won't keep its flavour long.

YOGHURT – any good variety will do, though we prefer real Greek yoghurt with this dish. ½ pint (300 ml) makes enough dressing for 4.

VEAL – not every butcher will know what a paillard is, indeed most cookery books don't mention the name, though there are paillards of salmon, too. However, the cut is the same as an escalope, beaten thin and quite large – as big as a soup plate, said one London butcher who did know. You needn't go to quite that size, but make sure the meat is free from fat and gristle, cut thin – about ¼ inch (5 mm) – and beaten thinner still, though not so hard that it begins to disintegrate, resembling mince rather than whole meat.

FRUIT FLAN – here you really will have to buy by eye, choosing what you fancy from what's on offer. Or could you order a flan from your local baker? In any case, try to find one made with fresh fruit rather than the canned variety. Ask how you should keep it – some fruit flans become rather liquid after a while, especially if they get too warm.

OTHER INGREDIENTS – a little olive oil to rub into the paillards, and a knob or two of butter for the vegetables.

WINE – grüner veltliner is Austria's native grape, dry and spicy (and so unaffected by the wine scandal that was all about sweetening wines). It's excellent as an aperitif, but has enough body to take you right through the meal, and is perfect for outdoor drinking too. Don't let the sometimes fancy names confuse you, but look for the name of the grape on the label, and the official Austrian seal of quality. Choose the youngest wine you can find and chill it well.

PREPARATION AND PRECOOKING

An hour before the appointed time, get your charcoal grill going if you are planning to eat outdoors – you will need it for a few minutes only to cook the paillards, but it must be very hot.

Make sure the wine is getting cold but take the meat from the refrigerator. Unwrap, lightly rub each paillard with a little olive oil on both sides, and let them warm separately on a flat surface.

Chop the ends from the cucumber, about 1 inch (2.5 cm) off each, and peel with a vegetable peeler. Save one or two long strips of the rind. Cut the cucumber in half lengthwise, and scrape out the seeds with a teaspoon. Do this gently, removing only the pips and watery core around them, so that you end up with two half tubes. Salt generously. Lay them side by side on a board, hollows down. With a sharp knife slice across into chunky semicircles about ⅛ inch (3 mm) thick. Put them in a colander and squeeze with your hands to remove as much liquid as you can, until the chunks look glassy and feel quite hard. Shake off the liquid. Place the colander with the cucumber in it in a soup plate or similar bowl, and return to the refrigerator. Cut the edges from the reserved cucumber rinds, chop into pieces about 1 inch (2.5 cm) long, and slice lengthwise again into fine strips for a little decoration to place on top of each serving. Store in the refrigerator.

Chop the chives very finely – 1 tablespoon per 2 servings.

Cut the top third from each artichoke, right through the globe, and discard. Pull off the hard outer leaves, and trim the stem to a remaining length of 1 inch (2.5 cm) or so. Quarter the globe and stem lengthwise; shorten the stem a little more if quartering reveals strings. With the point of the knife cut out and discard the fibrous choke over the delicate green disc at the bottom of the globe.

Wash the carrots in cold water, and top and tail. Leave them whole if they are no bigger than a little finger; otherwise cut them into long sticks, discarding hard cores.

Pod the peas.

Wash the spinach leaves in several changes of water, pull off long hard stems, and chop coarsely. Put to drain in a colander and set aside with the other vegetables.

Cut quarter wedges of lemon to serve with each paillard of veal.

COOKING AND PRESENTATION

If not using a charcoal grill, preheat an electric or gas grill to maximum heat.

Coat the bottom of a saucepan with water, put in the spinach leaves, and cook over low to medium heat, lid on, for 5 minutes. Add a knob of butter and stir until it has melted. Put the artichoke hearts and carrots on top, sprinkle with salt and black pepper, replace the lid, and reduce the heat to minimum.

Take the colander with the cucumber from the refrigerator, shake, and discard liquid. Put the chunks into a bowl, sprinkle with lemon juice, add the yoghurt and toss until evenly coated. Dust with sweet red paprika instead of pepper; don't add any more salt. Scatter the chopped chives and fine cucumber rinds on top.

Stir the vegetables, replace the lid, turn off the heat, and serve the first course with extra chives and paprika on the side.

Return the vegetables to low heat. Add the peas, 1-2 cloves of crushed garlic, a little more butter, and stir. Leave the lid off from now on. Heat a serving bowl with hot water from the tap or kettle.

Salt and pepper the paillards on one side only and put them seasoned side down on the charcoal grill, close to very hot embers – the bars should make the meat sizzle noisily, leaving strong brown grill marks on the surface. Season the top side and turn after 1 minute. Continue to grill for 1 more minute – 2 in all – and serve instantly, with a wedge of lemon. The meat should be barely pink inside.

If you are using an electric or gas grill, keep it at maximum temperature throughout, but season both sides of the meat first. Put the grid as close as possible to the heat; as with the charcoal, grill for 1 minute per side, turning only once.

Serve the vegetables in the preheated bowl.

Present the flan on a flat plate or dish, cutting at table.

SHOP AND SERVE

A mouth-watering shopping trip is almost all
you need do in preparation for this meal.

New radishes, with salt and chilled hard butter

*Fillets of smoked trout, with chunks of lemon and
rye bread*

*Jambon persillé and small meat pies from the
charcuterie counter*

*Salad of little spinach leaves, lettuce and spring
onions, with a mustard dressing*

Cheeses from central France

Simple French country wines
*Lager as an alternative with radishes and smoked
trout*

SHOPPING LIST

RADISHES – buy them pink and white, hard as bullets. Soft
radishes have either lost moisture, or may be woody inside, with
little taste. Count the radishes on an average bunch, and buy as
many per head as you might like to eat yourself for an appetizer,
with a little salt and butter to counter the sharpness. They
should be quite cold when served, so store in the salad tray of
the refrigerator.

SALAD – leave out the spinach if the leaves are big and unsightly, and substitute with frisé, cos or radicchio, it doesn't matter which – the idea is to create a hearty mix, crisp and crunchy among the meats and cheeses. Try to visualize the bowl you will be using to toss and serve the salad for your party in, then fill it about two thirds in your imagination for an idea of how much you need – buy generously, but be sparing with the spring onions, as not everyone finds them digestible.

LEMONS – a quarter wedge for each portion of smoked fish.

SMOKED TROUT – try to get a wild fish; go for the pink rather than the white-fleshed farmed variety, which can have the blandness of a convenience food. Sizes vary, of course, as do appetites. Imagine a helping in terms of sides or fillets. Leave the fish on the bone until you serve it. Store cold and well wrapped, or the smell might affect other things in the refrigerator.

JAMBON PERSILLÉ – a Burgundian galantine of raw ham and pig's trotters simmered in white wine and flavoured with parsley and garlic, traditionally made at Easter. Allow 1 good slice per person, and see if you can find some good English pies, Melton Mowbray for example, to accompany each helping.

CHEESES – a selection of cheeses from central France – bleu d'Auvergne, which resembles roquefort in size and shape though its taste is rather softer; cantal, one of France's oldest cheeses and not unlike cheddar; fourme d'Ambert, sometimes called fourme de Cantal, another, though sharper, blue from the same region; and Saint-Nectaire, a soft-pressed mountain cheese with a fragrant subtle flavour.

BUTTER – unsalted good quality butter for the radishes; allow 1 oz (25 g) per portion, and some more to go with the bread. Make sure to get it really cold.

MUSTARD – real Dijon makes a splendid dressing with groundnut or olive oil, but beware of the kind packaged especially for the UK market – it's sweeter than the original

French variety. English powdered mustard will serve well if given a little time to mature after you have mixed it.

OIL – groundnut makes a perfect mustard dressing, but strong olive oil may be nicer still. Whichever you use, be generous with it – count 1 tablespoon per head.

RYE BREAD – traditionally served with smoked salmon, rye bread would go well throughout this menu. Or, buy wholemeal or a variety of white and brown.

WINES – a hearty meal calls for hearty wines, young ones especially. Look for pink Corent and red Chanturgues, made with the gamay grape, if you want to stay with the Côtes d'Auvergne; or move a little further south, where your choice multiplies rapidly. Consider a glass of chilled lager with the radishes and smoked trout.

PREPARATION

There is little you can do in advance of this meal. If you are serving white, rose, a Gamay red or lager, make sure they are getting cold. Chill the butter for the radishes.

With half an hour or so to go, wash the radishes in cold water, top and tail them, but leave a little green as a handle on each. Sort through the spinach leaves, tear off and discard hard stalks, and rinse with several changes of cold water before you shake them dry. Here's a simple trick if you don't have a salad centrifuge – lay the leaves on a dry dish cloth, bundle up the ends so that the cloth forms a kind of pouch; then swing it in big full circles, overhead and down and up again, faster and faster. Don't make yourself uncomfortable – the centrifugal force will not only push the water into the cloth, but send more blood into your hand, which is why you might see a skier warm his frozen fingers in this way. Deal with the other leaves in similar fashion, top and tail the spring onions, and set it all aside in a cool place.

Make the mustard dressing now, especially if you intend using powdered mustard. With Dijon – put a tablespoon of it into a small mixing bowl, add a little black pepper if you like, but no salt. Pour in a little of the oil and whisk with a small wire whisk or fork until all the oil has been absorbed and you are beginning to get a glistening, creamy mix. Add more oil and mustard according to how much you need and how it tastes. Don't worry if the emulsion collapses after a while, you can soon whip it smooth again; put it in the refrigerator until you toss and serve the salad.

With powdered mustard – put the powder into a small mixing bowl, add a few drops of water and stir until all the water has been absorbed; add a little more water until the paste is quite smooth, without lumps. Let it sit for a while, 10 minutes or so, then proceed as with the Dijon.

PRESENTATION

You could of course lay out everything on the table at once, inviting your guests to help themselves, and be done. You might have more fun, though, if you served the meal in courses, beginning with a platter of the radishes, salt and cold butter. Serve only the white or pink wine at this stage, and offer cold lager as an alternative to offset the sharpness of the radishes.

Then serve the smoked trout, with wedges of lemon, and rye bread to be cut at table, with butter.

Offer the jambon persillé and meat pies next, with red wine for those who want a change. Bring in the salad, toss it at table, and finish with the cheeses.

SOUTHERN FLAVOURS

A meal for a party of six or so, and a day
when you have an hour to spare.

Dandelion and hot bacon salad

*Roast leg of lamb; white haricot beans in tomato
and basil sauce*

Sheep cheeses from Provence

*Red wine – a good cru beaujolais, such as a
Chiroubles or Julienas*

SHOPPING LIST

DANDELION – don't search the market for this simple salad, but
take a walk in the country, armed with a pointed knife and
basket. Choose little, tender leaves, which can be eaten down to
the connecting roots. Cut 3 good handfuls per portion and make
sure you don't let them dry out on your way home. Store in the
salad tray of the refrigerator. Little spinach leaves would be a
perfect alternative.

WHITE HARICOT BEANS – it's more or less impossible to tell the
age of dried beans until you are cooking them, so try to find a
shop with a good turnover and ask for new beans from the most
recent harvest. 1 lb (500 g) is plenty to serve with a leg of lamb big
enough for 6.

TOMATO SAUCE – for 6 helpings you will need about 1 lb (500 g)
canned or creamed tomatoes, reinforced with 1 teaspoon

tomato purée; ¼ pint (150 ml) olive oil; 1 medium onion; 2 cloves garlic; ½ tablespoon each dried thyme and oregano, doubled if fresh; 1 bay leaf.

BASIL – quite a few greengrocers in Britain sell fresh basil nowadays, either prepacked by the grower or as little plants that can live on in your kitchen for a while, offering better value than cut sprigs. Basil is mild in flavour and scented rather than tasty, so allow several leaves per head for the sauce. Store cut basil in the refrigerator.

LEG OF LAMB – telephone your butcher a few days in advance, telling him how many people you intend feeding. There is a bone in this cut of course, but almost everything else should be good lean meat, with little fat, so don't think of buying a whole leg if half will do. Choose indigenous fresh meat if possible. At home unpack and cover the leg loosely. Store it in the refrigerator if you are not going to cook it on the same day, otherwise leave it out.

BACON – buy green bacon, i.e. fresh unsmoked bacon that has been salted only, for the salad; allow ½ oz (15 g) per head.

SHEEP CHEESES – given the growing number of specialist shops in this country, you might just spot one or other of these cheeses from the south of France – rare cacha, tomme de Camargue scented with thyme and laurel, even brousse du Rove, a curd cheese sometimes eaten sugared with orange flower water. Alternatively, find out about domestic cheeses made with ewe's milk, for they too are growing in number and availability, from the pressed curd type flavoured with chives to full fat ones. Buy, by eye and taste if possible, enough to make an attractive and interesting offering. Store cheeses in the refrigerator only if you don't have another, better ventilated cool place. Cover the cut sides tightly, the other sides only loosely.

OTHER INGREDIENTS – olive oil for rubbing into the meat and frying the bacon; wine vinegar for the salad; salt and black pepper.

Wɪɴᴇ – Chiroubles and Julienas are two of the nine crus of the beaujolais that are best drunk when still relatively young. Try Moulin-à-Vent or Morgon if you prefer something a little more mature. You could serve a one- or two-year-old from the first group to begin with, followed by an older vintage from the second as you reach the cheese – three years should show quite a difference. Be generous with young beaujolais. Even moderate drinkers are tempted by the sheer quaffability of the gamay grape; allow half a bottle per person at least.

PREPARATION AND PRECOOKING

Beans – there are two ways of restoring moisture to dried beans, soaking in cold water overnight or covering them with boiling water from the kettle some 2-3 hours in advance. Choose whichever method suits your timetable, and cook them the night before if you like.

Drain off the soaking water and rinse the beans well to remove their indigestible substances.

The beans are cooked in the tomato sauce. Peel and finely chop 1 onion and 2 cloves of garlic. In a medium saucepan warm the olive oil, put in the onion and garlic and cook for 3-4 minutes, taking care not to burn the garlic or it will give a bitter taste. Add the soaked beans, stir, and cook for a further 5 minutes. Add the canned or creamed tomatoes, tomato purée, bay leaf, some pepper – but no salt or the beans will go hard and burst – and only ½ pint (300 ml) of water per pound (500 g) of beans. Put on the lid, bring to the boil and boil hard for 10 minutes, then cook slowly, for about 45 minutes, stirring occasionally – we use a heat diffuser over the lowest flame on our gas hob to keep the temperature right down. Add salt, test, and cook until done, when the beans should be soft inside with some resistance to the bite left – 1-1 ½ hours in all. You can let them cool now and store in a cool place overnight, or keep them hot, serving them with chopped fresh basil on top.

Big masses need disproportionately longer to heat or cool than small ones, so the heavier your leg of lamb, the more time it will take to warm up from the refrigerator if you kept it there – 3-4 hours if it's of medium size, depending also on the ambient temperature and how low the refrigerator was set, of course. Remove all excess fat from the surface of the meat. Rub with olive oil and let it sit in a suitable dish and place.

Work out your schedule for the lamb. Some older ovens need quite some time to get hot – i.e. to gas 8/450°F/230°C to begin with. Calculate 10 minutes cooking per pound (500 g) for pink, 12 for medium or 18 for well-done meat; add another 15 minutes regardless of weight to let the joint rest in a warm place before serving.

The younger the beaujolais the cooler – though never icy – we like to drink it. Put it in a cold room a few hours before the first guests are due; in the refrigerator, if necessary, for a little over half an hour or so.

Cut up the bacon for the dandelion salad into small squares. Heat a little olive oil in a frying pan and fry the bacon until golden brown. Set aside.

Last, sort through the dandelion leaves. Discard crushed or wilted greens, cut off the stems, and wash gently in several changes of cold water. Shake dry and set aside in a colander in a cool place.

COOKING AND PRESENTATION

Rub the leg of lamb with a little more olive oil, black pepper and salt. Place in a roasting tin, and put in the oven preheated to gas 8/450°F/230°C. Reduce to gas 4/350°F/180°C after 10 minutes, by which time the searing heat will have sealed the surfaces sufficiently to prevent the meat from drying out. Open the oven after 30 minutes, and spoon the juices in the roasting tin over the leg. Continue at the same moderate temperature, basting every now and then.

When the cooking time is up, turn the oven off and remove the leg, leaving the door wide open. Transfer it, meatier side on top, to a dish on which you can carve at table – flat enough not to restrict access, deep enough to collect the juices that will flow. Return the dish and meat to the warm oven, door ajar, to rest for 15 minutes – only then will the joint's flavour be fully developed.

While the lamb is resting, reheat the beans if necessary. Finely chop the basil leaves.

Finish off the dandelion salad. Heat a salad bowl with hot water from the kettle or tap, dry, and put in the greens. Reheat the bacon and olive oil and pour over the dandelion in the bowl. Quickly add a little wine vinegar to the frying pan, heat gently and stir, dissolving the meat deposits in the pan. Pour over the greens, sprinkle with fresh black pepper, toss, and serve immediately.

After the first course, put the beans in a serving bowl and sprinkle chopped basil on top.

Present the leg of lamb to your guests. Carve at table, serving straight on to individual plates. Steady the leg with the carving fork. Approximately at mid-length, make a deep incision down to the bone. Make a second cut at a slight angle towards the lowest point of the first, so that you get a thin slice – ⅛ inch (3 mm) thick or so – that you lift out. Repeat this on either side, gradually carving a widening V. Observe that the meat on the leg consists of different muscles and textures. Try to offer each guest a mixture of cuts, if not with the first serving, then with seconds.

HOT AND COLD

A picnic almost, for an early warm day.

Tortelli in butter and cream

*Cold roast chicken from the delicatessen counter;
green salad with tomatoes and wild fennel, with oil
and tarragon vinegar dressing*

Fresh pecorino cheeses from Tuscany

Cassata

*Galestro
Verdicchio*

SHOPPING LIST

TORTELLI – or tortellini or ravioli – fresh ones have been available in Soho shops for many years, and can be found in many delicatessens – there are now even special fresh pasta shops. We buy our *tortelli fatti in casa* from Lina's in Brewer Street in Soho. Make sure they have the right filling, though – ricotta and spinach rather than meat for this meal. For a starter allow 4 of the big (tortelli) variety per head, or 8 of the little ones (tortellini). Have them put in a box, transport carefully, and eat on the same day, though they will keep for a night in the refrigerator if absolutely necessary.

PECORINO – sheep cheese, made all over Italy, Sicily and Sardinia, mild when young, increasingly spicy with age. Ask for a fresh Tuscan cheese, but don't be put off if you are offered romano, for example. Try it. If you like it, buy some, judging quantity by eye; otherwise go for an altogether different choice – provolone, perhaps, which also grows from *dolce* to *piccante* as it matures.

BUTTER – ½ oz (15 g) of fresh slightly salted or unsalted butter per portion of pasta.

CREAM – allow 1 fl oz (25 ml) double cream per portion of pasta.

CASSATA – even in Italy nowadays restaurants rarely make their own variety of this iced confection, with a core of whipped frozen cream and chopped crystallized fruit, but rely on the manufactured variety, such as Motta or Alemagna. Allow about 4 oz (125 g) per helping. Buy it deep-frozen and get it home fast, into your own freezer, but look at the instructions about unfreezing first – should it go into the warmer refrigerator for a few hours in advance of serving?

CHICKEN – a whole cooked bird, weighing about 3 lb (1.5 kg), will feed 4. Don't be shy to ask when it was cooked – anything older than a day is likely to be dry, while the skin, which should be golden and crisp, will have become soggy, dark and limp. Try to buy on the day you will eat it. Store cold, covered loosely with a piece of foil or greaseproof paper.

SALAD – look for a buttery Webb's lettuce, with a yellow core that should be round, dense and cool in your hand. A good head will make enough salad for 4.

TOMATOES – ask for firm salad tomatoes; depending on size count 1-2 per portion.

WILD FENNEL – grows in many places in late spring, sometimes together with dill, with which it is said to cross-pollinate. A single good stem, which might be 3 feet (1 m) tall, may show enough leaves to dress your salad, but pick 2 or 3 stems if the leaves don't amount to a good handful. Keep in a vase of water, and pull off the leaves only when dressing the salad.

OLIVE OIL – buy some extra virgin from the first pressing if you don't have it in store already.

TARRAGON VINEGAR – wine vinegar infused with tarragon, a herb often used with chicken; Dufrais is a good, widely available make.

OTHER INGREDIENTS – fresh bread and butter for serving with the cheeses; salt and black pepper.

WINE – Galestro, as made by Antinori, Frescobaldi, Ricasoli and other big Tuscan houses who can afford the ultra-modern equipment needed to make this white wine from trebbiano and malvasia grapes. It's light in colour as well as alcohol – perfect, we believe, for a picnic or as a well-chilled aperitif on a hot day, though some critics deplore its neutrality. If you want a follow-up or a rather more characterful substitute from the beginning, look for Verdicchio dei Castelli di Jesi Classico from the Monte Schiavo co-operative – plain fresh Verdicchio of last year's vintage, or Pallio di San Floriano for a more powerful and sweeter wine.

PREPARATION

An hour or so before the meal make sure your wines are cool.

Check whether the cassata should be out of the freezer and in the refrigerator by now.

Take the lettuce from the refrigerator, discard the tough outer leaves, cut off remains of the root and look whether the rest actually needs washing, peeling off one leaf at a time. If washing is necessary, rinse under cold running water, shake, pull away discoloured sections if any, and put in a colander to drain. Return the leaves to the refrigerator for maximum crispness.

Rinse the tomatoes, dry, and keep with the lettuce.

Take the chicken from the refrigerator and let it lose its chill in a cool place.

Do the same for the tortelli. Put them on a board or big flat plate, and separate them if necessary along the perforated lines – by hand, not with a knife.

Work out how much water and the size of saucepan you will need to cook the tortelli – they ought to be able to move freely. Remember, 1 gallon (4.5 litres) of water, to which you should add 1 tablespoon of salt, may take 20 minutes to come to the boil, longer if not covered. Turn on the heat in good time – it's better to have simmering water standing by than have the timing thrown out because the water isn't ready.

COOKING AND PRESENTATION

Bring the water to the boil. Carefully slide the tortelli off their board and into the water. Let it come back to the boil and immediately reduce the heat to a gentle simmer – the tortelli will break if there is too much agitation. Cook with the lid off until they rise to the surface, 4 minutes or so, when they will be done.

Meanwhile put the double cream and butter in another saucepan big enough to hold the tortelli, stir and heat gently until the butter melts and the mix thickens.

When they are cooked, drain the tortelli through a colander or lift them out with a perforated spoon, and put them in the saucepan with the cream and butter. Toss gently until all are evenly covered. Portion them out on individual plates – soup plates, if you like – pour over the remaining sauce and serve directly.

Serve the cold chicken, salad and cheese together, but assemble the salad first. Cut the tomatoes into quarters if they are small or slice them, and put in a bowl big enough to let you toss freely. Take the lettuce from the refrigerator and add it to the bowl, tearing big leaves with your hands. Pick over the fennel leaves, chop them with a sharp knife, and distribute over the salad. Sprinkle with tarragon vinegar, a little salt and fresh black pepper. Pour over virgin olive oil and toss, preferably with your hands, until all the leaves feel smooth and glisten, evenly coated. Serve immediately.

Carve the chicken at table, on a board or flat dish. First find the joint between body and leg, and cut through it with the tip of the knife. Remove the wings in similar fashion. Slice the breast thinly on either side of the breast bone. Serve a mix of dark and white meats.

Offer the cheeses on a big plate, with fresh bread and butter on the side.

Serve the cassata, cutting it at table if it's a whole bombe.

SPRING FLAVOURS FROM THE SOUTH

Fish and meat, quickly done.

Grilled sardines

Carré d'agneau; green beans

Iced fresh pineapple maraschino

A young rosé from central or southern France

SHOPPING LIST

SARDINES – ask for small, unfrozen fish. As always, look for bright eyes, red rather than dull purple gills and a steely bluish shine on skins. Even fresh sardines are oily, with a smell that soon becomes overpowering. Have them cleaned, heads cut off, and wrapped up well for the transport home. Buy 2 or 3 per person.

CARRÉ D'AGNEAU – best end of neck – order new, indigenous lamb. Each *carré* or joint usually consists of 8 cutlets – even light eaters will want 2 each. Don't be talked into buying anything less than best end for this menu; it's better to have 2 small joints, with a maximum of 8 little cutlets each, than 1 big one, which may be not so tender and take longer to cook. Have joints trimmed French-style: rib ends exposed, scraped quite clean, and all but the bottom layer of fat removed. Though the butcher should know, make sure the chine bone is removed – otherwise you'll have to hack rather than carve the cutlets when serving.

GREEN BEANS – look for colour, beans should be green rather than the greyish colour often displayed, and fresh enough to snap with a clean break when broken. Reject pods which are thick or appear stringy with excessively curled, shrivelled tops and tails. Allow a little more than a good handful per person.

PINEAPPLE – sniff for the scent of a fruit approaching ripeness, but avoid fruit with mushy bruises hiding under the prickly outer skin. Imagine each guest will have 2 or even 3 slices a little under ½ inch (1 cm) thick, and you will have an approximate idea how big a fruit, or how many, you will need.

LEMON – you will need the juice of 1 lemon for the pineapple, plus a little for the beans and sardines.

HERBS – for the sardines – get a few sprigs of fresh oregano or marjoram, thyme and a little rosemary, plus a head of garlic.

WINE – a certain snobbery, in reaction perhaps to the notion that it amounts to nothing more than the compromise of the ignorant, too often advises against rosé. Yet, with a simple menu, where the fish will be flavoured with herbs and has a good strong taste of its own, why not serve a fresh pink wine throughout the meal? Here are three examples, none of them at all expensive, from different regions of France – Château de Fonscolombe, Côteaux d'Aix en Provence, VDQS; Rosé de Syrah, Domaine de Bosc, Vin de Pays de l'Hérault; Gris Fumé, Vin de Pays du Jardin de France.

MARASCHINO – a clear liqueur made from the marasca cherry, originally grown in Dalmatia, and scented with its kernels which add an almond flavour. It is tastier than most eaux-de-vie usually poured over fresh fruit and fruit salads. Look for a small bottle of Maraska from Zadar, traditionally square and wrapped in raffia, but beware of certain Italian liqueurs of low strength calling themselves *real* maraschino – they are nothing of the kind, and far too sweet. Use a little kirsch, if you can't get pure maraschino of proper strength. In either case, a single table-spoon would be enough for a whole pineapple of average size.

PREPARATION AND PRECOOKING

There is nothing much you need do in advance with this simple meal, though don't forget to chill the wine. Then, about an hour before your first guest is likely to arrive, take the lamb from the refrigerator and set the joint fat side up in a shallow baking tin. Let the meat warm towards room temperature.

Top and tail the beans. You can use kitchen scissors or a knife if you like, though many cooks use their fingernails – it's easier to detect strings, which should be pulled off, this way. Wash the beans in cold water and set aside in a colander.

Trim the pineapple. With a knife of good weight first cut away any leaves, and then the skin, working down in long strips. Slice across into discs perhaps ½ inch (1 cm) thick. Don't bother about coring – you lose less of the flesh this way, and the hard bits can always be left on the plate. Put the slices into a bowl, sprinkle with the juice of a lemon and add the maraschino or kirsch – 1 tablespoon or so. Turn the pineapple over several times, being careful not to break the discs. Put in the refrigerator.

Unwrap the herbs. Pick the thyme, marjoram and oregano leaves from their stems. Peel and coarsely chop the spring garlic.

Prepare the sardines. Take them from the refrigerator and rinse quickly. Dab dry with kitchen paper. Open up each fish, spreading them butterfly-fashion so they are quite flat. Lay them on a board or big plate, insides up. Pour a little olive oil over the insides and sprinkle with herbs. Set aside, ready for cooking except for pepper and salt.

COOKING AND PRESENTATION

Preheat the grill and oven to maximum temperature, i.e. gas 9/475°F/240°C for the oven.

Set water to boil for the beans, adding salt and a little lemon juice.

As your guests are about to sit down for the first course, put the lamb, fat side up as prepared, in the preheated oven, on the top shelf if it is not fan-assisted, otherwise anywhere provided it really does heat evenly. Reduce the heat to gas 6/400°F/200°C after 5 minutes. Cook for a total of 25 minutes for rare to medium-rare cutlets, and just 3 minutes more for medium ones.

To grill the sardines on a gas or electric grill, heat from above. Remove and oil the grid, and put on the fish, making sure they are lying really flat, open side up as you prepared them. When the grill is very hot, and your guests ready to eat at the table, put in the grid so that the sardines are no more than 2 inches (5 cm) from the heat. Watch all the time or you will overcook them – 3 minutes is ample for thinner fish. Serve and eat immediately. Offer chunks of lemon if you like.

When the lamb is done, switch off the oven. Take out the pan with the joint. Immediately return the joint to the oven on a plate or different pan, letting it rest inside, oven door slightly ajar.

Drop the beans into fast boiling water. Continue to cook at high heat but don't cover – if you do the extra heat from the steam will induce the chlorophyll in the beans to turn grey. Test after 5 minutes – they should still be firm to the bite when done, not mushy. Drain. Return to the still hot pan with a lump of butter, toss, turn into a serving bowl and bring to the table.

Take the lamb from the oven. Put the joint on a board, fat side down. With a sharp knife, carve the cutlets with one clean cut between each rib. Lay the cutlets on individual plates, mixing end and inside cuts according to preference. Serve immediately – the lamb really should be eaten hot.

Bring in the pineapple last. Offer a little more iced maraschino or kirsch on the side if you like.

LUXURY

This menu is quickly prepared and easy to adapt too; we prefer the avocado soup hot, but it lends itself well to chilling, and you could buy the lobster already cooked and eat it cold with a little mayonnaise. You will need a liquidizer or processor if you want to make the soup quickly, with a minimum of effort, but with a mouli or sieve it would take only a few minutes longer.

Avocado soup

Lobster with hot butter

Salad of new potatoes, mange-touts and mushrooms

A selection of soft English cheeses served with slices of iced melon

A fresh white wine made from sauvignon grapes, such as a Sancerre or Pouilly Fumé, which you could compare with a related Californian Fumé Blanc towards the end of the meal

SHOPPING LIST

Avocados – big waxy green pears may look tempting, but can be insipid and too bland even for soup. Crinkly, dark, small avocados with deliciously creamy flesh of a nutty fragrance are our favourites, a variety grown in countries as far apart as Israel and Mexico – 2 big specimens will make 4 generous portions of soup, 6 at a pinch. Begin your search in good time, though, a few days in advance – because they have to travel so far, avocados usually arrive as hard as bullets here, and there are times when no greengrocer may have a single ripe fruit. Avoid specimens that immediately feel soft and squishy under the skin, as they are probably over-ripe and brown inside, with a bitter flavour that won't go away even in soup.

OTHER INGREDIENTS FOR THE SOUP – for the quantity of soup described, i.e. 4-6 portions, you will need ¼ pint (150 ml) double cream and 3 chicken stock cubes.

LEMONS – half a fruit to acidulate the water for the mange-touts; depending on size and acidity, count an extra half to dress the salad; plus a quarter per guest to offer finger bowls when eating the lobster if you like.

NEW POTATOES – buy Italian or Spanish for this salad, Jerseys only if reasonable in price. Ask for small potatoes, so that 3 or 4 make a handful for each serving.

MANGE-TOUTS – or snow peas – which you can eat with their pods. Look for bright green pods, which should be whole and quite flat. As with potatoes and mushrooms buy by eye rather than weight – a good handful per person will do.

MUSHROOMS – buy closed cap mushrooms, which are a little bigger than button mushrooms, and have a wilder flavour. Avoid leathery, wrinkling skins, which indicate loss of moisture – consistency and texture are important in this salad. Reject broken caps or specimens with stems missing. Count 1 or 2 depending on size per portion.

MELONS – canteloupe, ogen and honeydew are but three of the varieties reaching us from different parts of the world at most times of the year. Some greengrocers will press their thumbs into the button mark opposite the stem, which is the weakest point of any melon, until it softens whatever its true state, but be guided by your nose – don't buy if you can't catch at least a whiff of aroma. Allow for 2 thinnish slices per head. At home rinse the melon, dry, and put in the refrigerator, where it will take several hours to chill right through. Look for pears if you're not sure the melons on offer are all right – but they, too, are ripe only if they smell so.

LOBSTER – ring your fishmonger a few days in advance and order a small lobster per person, weighing no more than 1 lb (500 g) each. Ask for live lobsters – your best guarantee that they will be fresh. If you have a choice pick lively rather than sluggish specimens. Take them home quickly. Loosely wrapped in damp newspaper, lobsters can survive the better part of a day if kept in a cool place. Alternatively order the lobsters already done and serve them cold with mayonnaise – many fishmongers boil their own and will do so on request.

BUTTER – allow at least 1 oz (25 g) of top quality unsalted for each lobster.

OLIVE OIL – a few tablespoons of extra virgin olive oil for the salad, but rather more if you are going to make mayonnaise to accompany cold lobsters. See Menu 14 (p. 82) for quantities and instructions.

CHEESES – buy a small choice of 2 or 3 soft white cheeses to serve with the slices of chilled melon. For example, compare a plain coulommiers-type cheese made with English cow's milk with one made with that of ewe's. Consider adding an indigenous soft goat's cheese for extra taste and interest. In any case, ask, see and taste what's available, and buy as fresh and late as possible, deciding on quantities by eye.

WINES – we tried two sauvignons one night when invited to dinner, with salmon, though, not lobster. The first was a 1984 Sancerre, Domaine les Beauregards, the second a slightly more expensive 1984 Pouilly Fumé, Les Chantallouettes; everyone liked the first rather better, the second being judged rather sharp and thin by comparison. A few days later we discovered the same two wines in the result of a blind tasting held by WINE magazine, pleased to see we had been right – our favourite had won three stars, the dearer Pouilly Fumé only two. However, the story really begins here, for, quite apart from some rather depressing observations as regards the chances of picking good Sancerre or Pouilly Fumé from anyone's shelf, the editor revealed that three non-French sauvignons had been included in the tasting, and that they, had their "phenomenally high marks" been allowed to stand, would have been the winners – Cloudy Bay, a New Zealand wine, came top; Montana's Sauvignon, also from New Zealand and very cheap into the bargain, did almost as well; while Robert Mondavi's Californian Fumé Blanc, which is rather sweeter, was also in the top group.

PREPARATION AND PRECOOKING

Some 2 hours in advance, wash the potatoes, scrubbing their skins with a hard brush. Choose a saucepan and put in water – the potatoes will need to be well covered, but don't put them in yet. Add a little salt, cover and place on a high heat. When the water is boiling, drop in the potatoes, let it come back to the boil, and reduce to a lively simmer. Test after 12 minutes. Drain the potatoes when they are done, put them in the bowl you will be serving the salad from, and pour over lemon juice so that they get well coated. Add plenty of virgin olive oil, a little salt and black pepper. Toss while still very hot, then set aside to cool, turning them every now and then.

Meanwhile rinse the mange-touts and snap off their tops, pulling away the strings with them, if any. Discard limp or otherwise unsightly pods. In a saucepan big enough to hold them comfortably, bring plenty of salt water to a fast boil. Add the juice of half a lemon, wait for the froth to dissolve, and plunge in the mange-touts for 2 minutes at full heat, lid off. Drain immediately, rinse under cold water to stop further cooking, let drip, and set aside in a cool place.

Pick over the mushrooms next. Make sure you have a sharp knife for what follows – the cleaner your cuts, the better your salad will look and taste. Cut sandy ends off the stems and remove ragged skin around the edges of the caps, but don't peel them. Gently rinse the mushrooms under cold water, being careful not to get their gills soggy. Cut one in half lengthwise, through the cap and stem. Continue slicing the halves in the same direction, so that you end up with mushroom shapes approximately ¹⁄₁₆ inch (1.5 mm) thick. Set them aside with the mange-touts and potatoes, but don't assemble the salad now.

Check the temperature of the wine. Incidentally, fresh sauvignons make excellent aperitifs, on their own as well as sweetened with a little blackcurrant liqueur or crème de cassis – a thimble per glass does the trick, and works in some light red wines as well, when a kir becomes a cardinal in France.

If you are serving the lobsters cold, make the mayonnaise as described on page 85 to go with them.

Work out the rest of your timetable: the soup will take only a few minutes and is best prepared at the last moment unless you want to chill it, in which case it should go into the refrigerator about 3 hours in advance; the salad is almost made; the cheese and fruit can be got ready just before serving; but you'll need boiling water by the time you sit down to the first course – even 2 lobsters of the size described require something of the order of 1 gallon (4.5 litres) of water, which may take up to 20 minutes to come to the boil. Find a suitable saucepan, fill it, add plenty of salt – think of sea water, which is excellent for cooking fish – cover with a lid, and turn it on in good time.

COOKING AND PRESENTATION

Make the soup as your guests are settling with their aperitifs – it will take no more than 5 minutes.

For the quantities described, boil 1¾ pints (about 1 litre) of water. Put the chicken stock cubes in a saucepan and dissolve with a little boiling water. Pour in the rest of the water, stir, and set aside for a moment to cool. Cut the avocados in half, discard the stones and scoop out the flesh into a food processor or liquidizer. Add the cream, and process until smooth. Add 1 ladleful of the stock and process again briefly. Pour the mix into the saucepan containing the rest of the stock. Set on a low heat, correct with a little salt and fresh black pepper, whisk until all is creamy, and serve without delay.

If you want to chill the soup, let it cool, then cover with a lid or cling film to prevent discoloration and refrigerate for 3 hours or so. Whisk the soup for a moment or two before serving in individual bowls.

Drop the lobsters into fast boiling water as you are about to sit down to eat the first course – they will take 10 minutes to cook, uncovered.

After the first course, melt the butter for the lobsters – 2 walnut-sized knobs each – in a small saucepan. Get the butter hot but don't burn it – it should be clear gold, not brown. Warm a sauce boat or small jug with hot water for bringing it to the table.

There's only one way of eating hot lobsters with melted butter – mainly by hand. Offer finger bowls, with a wedge of lemon each, plus a jug of warm water to pour from and some extra paper napkins.

Take the lobsters from the boiling water – their heat will dry them instantly. Unless you have enough of the right imple-ments for breaking the claws at table, crack them now – taps rather than blows with a hammer or rolling pin should do. Serve the lobsters on a platter, which can also be used for the empty shells. (Our friend Frank Arsenault, who grew up in Maine, where lobsters are more plentiful than anywhere else, and to whom we are indebted in spirit for this menu, has more radical ideas – for a lobster feast lay the table with a paper cloth, so that at the end you can remove empty plates, glasses and cutlery, leave all debris on the table, roll the whole thing up, and discard.)

At table, pull off the legs – they're thinnest and will cool first, so suck them now, as appetizers so to speak. Next open the claws and eat them with a little hot butter. Straighten the tail and twist, gently pulling it from the body – if you're lucky the flesh will come out all in one go. Otherwise make an incision along either edge of the underside, break away the softish cover and lift out the tail. Gently prise the flesh open lengthwise to expose the intestine, which you discard, together with the black stomach sac at its upper end just inside the body. You can find some delicious things in there, too – the creamy green tomalley and orange roes, if the lobster is female – but first enjoy the tail.

If you decided to buy the lobsters cold, proceed as described or ask the fishmonger to split them in half. Serve with mayonnaise.

Make the salad when the table has been cleared. Put the mange-touts with the potatoes. Pour on a little more lemon juice and rather more olive oil, sprinkle with a little salt and fresh black pepper, and toss gently until everything is evenly coated. Add the mushrooms last, scattering them over the top – even without tossing they will have absorbed enough of the dressing by the time they reach individual plates.

After the salad take the melon from the refrigerator, cut it in quarters with a sharp knife, discard the pips (though you could toast them some other time, with a little salt), and take off the rinds. Arrange on a big plate and serve with the cheeses.

ARISTA FIORENTINA

A popular classic, suitable for small and big parties, with less to be done than might appear at first sight.

Tomato and mozzarella salad

Arista Fiorentina – roast loin of pork Florentine-style; cannellini beans in olive oil

First peaches, apricots and nectarines of the season

Chianti Classico or Rufina

SHOPPING LIST

MOZZARELLA – even outside Italy the real fresh article, made with buffalo milk, can be found nowadays. It's relatively expensive though, and worth the extra money only if really fresh; if it isn't fresh, settle for the the cow's milk variant – it, too, is delicious when in good condition. Mozzarella for eating uncooked is formed into small white balls, which, traditionally, are wrapped in paper and kept immersed in bowls of water until sold; 1 cheese will make a generous salad for 2 people. Store wet as in the shop, in the refrigerator if your larder is not cool enough, but only keep for a day or two or the cheese will go on developing, turning rubbery and yellow in the process.

VIRGIN OLIVE OIL – for the mozzarella as well as for the roast loin and beans, so make sure your supplies are not too low; allow 1 tablespoon per starter and the same again per portion of beans.

TOMATOES – look for salad tomatoes approximately the same size as mozzarella cheeses, i.e. half a tennis ball. Choose firm fruit. Count 1 per person.

PEACHES, APRICOTS AND NECTARINES – look around and ask what's new on the market, and ripe, for peaches and nectarines especially can look ripe while their insides are still hard. Apricots deepen in colour, with a pink hue and specks, as they reach maturity. Buy by eye, counting 1 peach and nectarine per person with a few apricots in addition.

GARLIC – buy a bulb of spring garlic to season the meat.

ROSEMARY – get a few sprigs.

SAGE – a good handful of leaves for the meat, but double that for additional decoration if you decide to cook the roast boned and rolled.

CANNELLINI BEANS – ask for new beans from the most recent harvest. Don't let anyone tell you that dried beans keep forever – they may keep but will fall apart as you attempt to cook them until soft, rendering themselves inedible. Ideally they should be of the last harvest within the year, though even the shopkeeper may not be sure just how old they are. 4 oz (125 g) makes 2 helpings.

LOIN OF PORK – even a small butcher usually has more than one of this prime cut in store, so you should not need to order in advance unless you intend feeding more than 6 people, in which case it may be better to buy 2 small loins rather than 1 very big one. This dish is extremely good, some would say even better eaten cold, so leftovers need certainly not go to waste. Ask the butcher to show you a loin. If it's from the fore or middle loin, the ribs are likely to be still attached. Imagine that each represents a chop, equivalent to 1 portion, and you will be able to judge by eye how much to buy.

There are two simple ways of cooking this classic Florentine roast, on or off the bone: the first may give a little more flavour – there are many who hold that the best meat is that closest to the bone, and cooked on it – whereas the second, with the loin boned, rolled and tied, can be carved more thinly, and may be the more elegant way of portioning out and serving this dish. Whichever method you decide on, insist on a piece of even thickness over its entire length. Ask the butcher to remove the rind, leaving only a thin layer of fat underneath. If you are going to cook the loin on the bone, ask him to chine it as well, so that you can carve it into chops at table. Otherwise have it boned, rolled and tied – a standard request that should take no more than a few minutes to carry out.

WINE – Chianti Classico or Rufina is the obvious choice to accompany a classic Tuscan roast – look for a 1981 Riserva, from Brolio, Villa Antinori, or Castello di Nippozzano. Alternatively, why not be a little adventurous and choose one of the single or nearly single grape wines made by some of the same top growers of the region? Look for a rather more mature vintage – Castello di Volpaia's Coltasala, Villa di Capezzana's Carmignano Riserva or Antinori's Tignagnello, for example.

PREPARATION

Unless you actually are in Tuscany or a country where cannellini are grown and you know that they are quite quite new, in which case they don't need soaking at all, put the cannellini beans in cold water overnight, or pour boiling water over them some 2-3 hours before the meal.

At the same time, i.e. 2 hours in advance, take the loin from the refrigerator. Whether it's on the bone or not, set it in a roasting tin, fat side up. Crush some cloves of garlic with a knife blade. Strip 2-3 sprigs of rosemary of their leaves. Pour some olive oil and rub it all over the meat, adding the crushed garlic, rosemary and a handful of the sage, both of which you must first crumple a little to release their full flavour. If the loin has been rolled, you can decorate it with whole sage leaves, sticking them down on the fat upper side in between the lines made by the string.

Take the mozzarella from its water, unwrap and put on a board. Moisten the blade of a sharp knife and slice the cheese carefully, about ⅛ inch (3 mm) thick. Do the same with the tomatoes, producing slices of similar size and thickness as those of the cheese. Take individual flat plates, salad or dining size. Except for the rims sprinkle them with salt. Carefully pour olive oil over the salt until the oil has spread evenly to the inside of the rims – the salt should stay at the bottom, not swim. Now lay a tomato slice on the first dish, touching on the inside of the rim. Put a mozzarella slice half over it, followed by one of the tomato, until you get to the other side and you have an interleafing row of red and white – half a mozzarella and a whole tomato making one starter. Keep to this pattern if you like it, or make up your own, and repeat as required.

Set the plates aside in a cool place, ready to be served. Add fresh black pepper only at table; if necessary point out that there is salt on the plates already. There should be no need for lemon juice or vinegar – even northern tomatoes usually have enough of their own acidity for this gentle salad.

Last, work out the cooking times – the loin will take 20 minutes per pound (500 g) if on the bone; about 22 minutes if off the bone; plus 15 minutes irrespective of size for the joint to rest before serving. The beans may need 40 minutes to 1 hour to cook.

COOKING AND PRESENTATION

Preheat the oven to gas 6/400°F/200°C. Except for the fatty upper side, once again rub the joint with the oil, garlic and herbs, but then remove the bigger pieces of garlic and the rosemary leaves as they would turn bitter in the heat. Sprinkle with plenty of salt and place the roast on the top shelf. Reduce the heat to gas 3/325°F/160°C after 10 minutes, and continue to roast for the remaining time. There is no need to baste – the fat running from the top will keep the sides moist. When the cooking time is up, turn off the heat, remove the loin and leave the oven door open. Put the meat on a suitable dish and return to oven, door ajar.

Meanwhile place the roasting tin with the cooking juices on low heat, skim off most of the fat with a spoon, add a splash of water or good wine, stir with a wooden spoon to loosen bits stuck to the pan and let simmer for a moment. Heat a sauce boat or suitable small jug with hot water and serve the sauce you just made in that. Carve the meat at table – into chops if on the bone, or rather thinner slices if the loin has been rolled.

Depending on their freshness, which, ultimately, only cooking will reveal, the beans may need little more than 40 minutes to cook. However, it's obviously better not to take such freshness for granted, so begin a little earlier. An hour before the appointed time, drain the beans, rinse them well, put them in a saucepan, cover with water and bring to the boil quickly, lid on. Do not add salt at this stage or the skins will break and the insides go hard. Remove the lid when the water is boiling. Boil hard for 10 minutes, then reduce the heat so that the water does not move too fiercely, as this, too, will damage the skins. Begin testing after 30 minutes. Add only 1 teaspoon of salt – you can always add more later, to individual tastes. Drain when done – there should be some resistance to the bite left – and return to the saucepan, lid on, to keep warm if necessary, though cannellini beans will taste just as good tepid or cold. Serve with fresh black pepper and a small jug of virgin olive oil on the side – that's how the Tuscans eat this dish, each adding a little oil to his or her taste.

Arrange the fruit on a big plate and serve it before the coffee, with a bowl of cold iced water to rinse it in.

GREEN AND WHITE

But with accents of yellow and other colours,
and a variety of textures and flavours, too;
almost entirely prepared in advance and
easily adapted in terms of numbers.

Smoked halibut

Fresh white tagliatelle with asparagus and cream

Stewed apricots and prunes

Gewürztraminer

SHOPPING LIST

SMOKED HALIBUT – light, white, half the price of smoked salmon but with plenty of class, this is a northern delicacy well worth looking for. Buy it thinly sliced, imagining it laid out on individual plates – 4 oz (125 g) may be enough for 2 people. At home put it in the refrigerator even if you are planning to serve it soon – it's good with a slight chill.

LEMONS – a quarter per starter; choose slightly under-ripe bright yellow fruit to give an accent to this simple starter.

ASPARAGUS – allow 4 bright green sticks per person, more if not perfect and of good size. Above all make sure the tips are intact, and look at the cut ends – the drier and harder they appear the more you may have to discard. Gently rinse the cut ends under cold water when you get the asparagus home, removing loose earth and sand; let drip, wrap in a damp cloth, and store in a cool place – the refrigerator if necessary.

SHALLOT – 1 will enhance the flavour of 2 portions of asparagus sauce.

TAGLIATELLE – only the fresh white variety will do justice to fresh asparagus. Unless you do it frequently, it's difficult to judge quantities of uncooked pasta by eye; 6 oz (175 g) makes a generous helping, 4 oz (125 g) an acceptable one for smaller appetites. Transport your purchase carefully, without other things on top. Store in a freezer bag in the refrigerator if necessary – for up to 4 days if it was fresh in the first place.

CREAM – one ¼ pint (150 ml) pot of single cream is plenty for 2 helpings.

DRIED APRICOTS AND PRUNES – stewed, these make one of the most delicious and easily prepared puddings we know; it keeps very well in the refrigerator – for up to 2 weeks – so make a lot each time you prepare it. Buy 1 lb (500 g) of each to feed up to 8 people. You also need for that quantity of fruit 12 fl oz (350 ml) good red wine; 10 oz (300 g) of soft brown sugar; 2 cinammon sticks; the peel from 1 large lemon.

OTHER INGREDIENTS – fresh rye bread to serve with the halibut, if you like.

WINE – gewürztraminer may be the grape to take you into and through part of this meal, starting with a fresh young wine and ending with an older, richer vintage. You could compare different areas that grow this spicy (hence *gewürz*) grape – South Tirol, where the village of Tramin lent its name to it; the Veneto and Friuli; even New Zealand or Australia; and, praised above all, Alsace. Be sure of variety, though – at times it's as if this particular grape's very spiciness causes taste buds to resign. Change to a red wine with the main course, perhaps the one you used to stew the apricots and prunes, if you want to take a different, and maybe safer route.

PREPARATION AND PRECOOKING

Make the stewed fruit a day or two in advance, even longer if you like, quantities as given in the shopping list or in proportion. With a vegetable peeler, thinly pare the rind from the lemon; put the red wine and the same volume of water into an enamelled or stainless steel pan; add the lemon peel, cinammon sticks and brown sugar; bring to the boil uncovered, turn down the heat, and let simmer for 5 minutes. Add the dried apricots and prunes and simmer for an additional 15 minutes, lid on. Let cool, transfer the whole into a glass jar with an airtight lid, and refrigerate.

Apart from the pudding only the asparagus needs to be pre-pared a little in advance of this meal. Lay the sticks on a board, chop off the dry bottom ends – 1 inch (2.5 cm) or so – and discard. Pick up a stick, tip pointing at you. With a small sharp knife loosen a strip of the hard top layer of skin you can see around the cut end. Pull it towards the tip, but note how it thins and ends well before – in other words, only the lower part of an asparagus stalk needs a little peeling if it's not to be eaten by hand. Peel all of the sticks.

In a saucepan big enough to hold the asparagus lying down, put enough water to cover but not drown them. Add a little salt, cover, and bring to the boil, lid on. When the water is boiling fast, squeeze in a little lemon juice to help preserve the green of the asparagus, and carefully drop in the sticks, cut ends first. Reduce the heat to a lively simmer, lid off. Test a stick after 10 minutes – even the bottom end should be nearly done. Turn off the heat and lift the asparagus out now, spreading the sticks on a double layer of kitchen paper – you will finish cooking them later. Keep the water, to add to that for the tagliatelle. When the sticks have cooled a little and shed their excess liquid, chop them into pieces approximately 1 inch (2.5 cm) long.

Peel the shallot, chop it fine, and put into a frying pan or shallow saucepan big enough to hold the cut pieces of asparagus, but don't add them now. Pour in half a glass of your wine – the one you will be drinking with this course, white or red – and simmer gently, stirring every now and then, until most of the liquid has gone. (Use a whole glass of wine for 3 or more shallots.) Season with a little salt and let cool, ready for the final stage.

Don't forget to heat the water for the pasta in time – we repeat it perhaps too often, but a gallon (4.5 litres) of water can take up to 20 minutes to come to the boil. At the other extreme, if it is white, is the wine you just used chilled enough?

COOKING AND PRESENTATION

Serve the smoked halibut laid out on individual plates, with a quarter lemon each. Offer fresh black pepper on the side, with rye bread if you like.

Warm up a bowl big enough to serve the pasta from, in a low oven or with hot water.

Allow at least 1 gallon (4.5 litres) of water, including that used for the asparagus, to cook 1 lb (500 g) of fresh tagliatelle. Don't add any more salt. Bring the water to a fast boil.

Meanwhile put the pan with the prepared shallot on low to medium heat. Add a generous knob of butter, enough to cover the bottom once it has melted. When the butter is beginning to turn colour, carefully drop in the asparagus, pour the cream over and stir gently, or rather, turn the asparagus pieces, so that they get coated and heat through evenly. Continue for 4-5 minutes.

Drop the pasta into the boiling water; it will sink to the bottom. Stir once or twice to make sure nothing sticks, let the water come back to the boil, and watch the tagliatelle rise. Taste one – home-made pasta cooks within a couple of minutes, 5 at the most. Drain through a colander, shake gently and turn into the preheated serving bowl.

Season the asparagus and cream with a little salt and fresh black pepper and pour straight onto the piping hot tagliatelle. Serve immediately.

Last, offer the stewed dried fruit, then coffee.

SUMMER

FOR IN OR OUT OF DOORS

A light and cool menu, with a minimum of advance preparation, suitable for indoor or outdoor eating.

Iced cucumber soup

Grilled poussin; baby carrots and new peas in butter

Watercress and mushroom salad, with walnut oil and lemon dressing

Raspberries

Vinho Verde

SHOPPING LIST

Poussin – call your butcher or poulterer a few days in advance to ask whether he can get you free-range poussins for the day you want to cook them, small enough to serve 1 bird per person; though you could go one size up to double poussins or spring chickens, 1 for 2 helpings. Ask for the birds to be flattened, so that you can grill them; alternatively flatten them yourself as described later.

Cucumber – a medium one will make 4 helpings of iced soup (a really large one 6). Look for a firm ripe specimen, dark rather than pale to get the full flavour. Make sure the skin is undamaged – peeling is not required for this recipe. Wash, wipe and put in the refrigerator as soon as you get the cucumber home.

OTHER INGREDIENTS FOR THE SOUP – for 4 servings you will need 1 clove of garlic; 1 large gherkin; 1 tablespoon tarragon vinegar; salt; ¼ pint (150 ml) each of double cream, sour cream and yoghurt; a few fresh mint leaves.

CARROTS – small ones, no bigger than a small finger, with fresh spicy foliage. A handful per helping.

PEAS – look at the pods – are they bulging and speckled? In that case even fresh peas are likely to be hard and bitter. Choose somewhat slimmer pods, which ought to be bright green and snap open easily in your fingers. Compared with the carrots, they are not quite so easy to judge in terms of quantity, but 2 handfuls should be about right for 1 helping. Small courgettes could be an alternative for this menu.

WATERCRESS – a bunch per person, provided that it's crisp and fresh.

MUSHROOMS – buy white round buttons, the cleaner and more compact the better, for then not only will their texture and taste be superior, but your work, too, will be easier. A handful per helping.

LEMON – for the salad dressing; half will dress a salad for 4 people. Also, a lemon for dressing the raspberries.

RASPBERRIES – unless you can pick your own, take a good look at what's on offer in the market. Raspberries are so soft they will squash under their own weight once they have been picked and continue to ripen. Punnets are used to keep pressure off, but even then layers of mush often hide at the bottoms of containers filled more than a day ago. So buy as fresh and late as possible, on the day you will eat them. At home empty the punnets and spread the berries in a shallow bowl. Even for a short while store them in the refrigerator.

DRIED HERBS – a shallow handful to rub each poussin with before grilling.

BUTTER – for the carrots and peas. Calculate 1 oz (25 g) per portion.

WALNUT OIL – a little will go a long way, for this oil is light and spreads well. Ask if the oil is from a recent pressing – it might be rancid otherwise, especially if it was kept on a warm shelf. Buy only a little container, indigenous or foreign. Store in the refrigerator.

OTHER INGREDIENTS – some caster sugar to dress the raspberries, if you like.

WINE – Vinho Verde is green wine from northern Portugal, but don't be misled; though little exported, some 60 % are red, for *verde* describes not the colour but its fresh style, as opposed to *maduro*. An association of producer-bottlers was formed early in 1985, with the declared policy of making limited quantities of wine from own grapes only, and in due course we should be able to find even Palacio de Brejoeira, famous for its white wines made from the alvarinho grape alone, on British shelves. Gatão is a brand which we have been enjoying meanwhile. Look for Dão Grão Vasco or Ribatejo Dom Hermano as white, more southern, alternatives if you can't find a good Vinho Verde.

PREPARATION

The soup needs to be made first, so that it will be cold enough when you serve it, though you can save cooling time if you work quickly with cold ingredients. Even then allow at least 1 hour for the soup to compose itself in the refrigerator.

Cool a soup terrine or other suitable bowl with ice cubes and water. Crush the garlic with a knife blade, and finely chop the gherkin. Wash but don't peel the cucumber, shred it quickly as thin as you can and put it in the terrine, having discarded the cooling liquid first. Add the garlic, chopped gherkin, tarragon vinegar and a little salt. Put in the double and sour creams and the yoghurt, stir until smooth and put in the refrigerator. Leave the mint for later.

Make sure the wine is getting cold and remove the poussins from the refrigerator. They ought to be reaching room temperature by the time you grill them. Flatten them if the butcher or poulterer has not done so already – put a bird on a board, back down; from the open neck, insert a heavy knife with a big blade, and break and cut through the back bone; open up the sides, and with the heel of your hand flatten the poussin by pushing down the breast. Rub it with a little olive oil, dried herbs, salt and pepper. If you are going to barbecue, start your fire in good time.

Discard greens and wash the carrots in cold water, scrubbing with a hard brush if necessary. Top and tail with a knife, but leave them whole if they are really small. Otherwise cut into matchsticks, discarding hard cores.

Shell the peas. Set them aside, but don't mix with the carrots at this stage.

Wash the watercress in several changes of cold water. Cut and discard long stalks. Dry in a salad centrifuge, or wrap in a clean cloth and swing vigorously. Set aside in a cool place.

Quickly rinse the mushrooms, dab dry with kitchen paper, trim stems, and slice vertically – i.e. into mushroom shapes, as thin as you can. Blunt knives bruise and damage textures – the cleaner your cuts, the better your salad will look and taste. Cover with a damp cloth and set aside in a cool place.

COOKING AND PRESENTATION

Preheat an electric or gas grill to medium temperature. Alternatively, check your barbecue is reaching the stage where you have an even spread of embers covered with grey ashes.

Take the cucumber soup from the refrigerator and taste; season with salt and a little black pepper if necessary. Decorate with a few leaves of mint and serve immediately.

Once more rub the poussins with olive oil, herbs and a little salt and pepper, and place on or under the grill, at medium heat and not too close, open side towards the fire. Watch this process carefully – if the meat burns, turn it at once, and increase the distance a little; baste before turning again, and keep on basting until the skin on the uncut side, i.e. the breast, is of an even golden brown. The whole process should take approximately 12 minutes.

Meanwhile melt a good knob of butter in a saucepan, add the carrots, stir and cook over low to medium heat until they begin to soften. Add a little more butter, the peas and salt. Stir occasionally. Serve as soon as the poussins are done.

Make the salad at table, after you have finished the main course if you wish. First, put the watercress only in the salad bowl. Pour in walnut oil, sprinkle with lemon, a little salt and fresh black pepper, and toss until all the leaves glisten and are evenly coated. Scatter the cut mushrooms over the top, and serve directly before they get soggy with the dressing.

Serve the raspberries, sprinked with lemon juice and a little sugar.

A GREAT SOUP

Minestrone does not only mean a big soup, as
indicated by the suffix *-one* joined to what
otherwise would be simple *minestra*. It's also
one of the most varied and exciting soups we
know, best served as a main dish,
hot or cold.

Minestrone with pesto

Grilled crottin de Chavignol

Red, white and black cherries

*Marzemino Trentino or Teroldego Rotaliano
Sancerre*

SHOPPING LIST

A proper minestrone is a convivial dish, best made for a party, so
here are the ingredients for 8 good helpings, but don't worry if
you can't find one or the other – substitute whatever is good and
fresh on the market. All quantities are approximate.

GREENGROCERIES – 1 large Spanish onion; 4 cloves of new garlic –
2 for the soup, 2 for the pesto; 8 oz (250 g) carrots, no bigger than
a small finger if possible; 8 oz (250 g) new potatoes, small enough
so that 3 or 4 make a handful, alternatively make do with slightly
bigger ones and cut them in half; 8 oz (250 g) French beans; 1 lb
(500 g) spinach; 1 lb (500 g broad beans; 1 lb (500 g) peas; 8 oz (250
g) courgettes; 2 leeks; 4-5 stalks of celery; 1 bunch of parsley; a

bay leaf; 1 sprig each of thyme, oregano, sage and mint – fresh if possible, otherwise dried from the grocer; 2 basil plants for the pesto, about 6 inches (15 cm) tall with good foliage.

CHERRIES – look around and see what's on the market; cherries come in all sorts of colours, from ivory pink through bright red to nearly black, and flavours from sweet to sour. Not a few of them are grown in England, with Kent White Hearts a popular favourite. Buy by taste and eye, and a lot if the quality is right – good cherries last but a very short time, and you might have to wait a whole year before you have another chance of enjoying them.

GROCERIES – 8 oz (250 g) dried cannellini or borlotti beans from the most recent harvest; 4 oz (125 g) split peas; 4 oz (125 g) barley; 4-5 rashers of bacon (optional); 1 lb (500 g) can of Italian tomatoes; 1 tablespoon tomato purée; a glassful of good quality red wine (about ¼ pint/150 ml); 4 oz (125 g) dried pasta shells or spaghetti; 8 oz (250 g) pine nuts; 4 tablespoons of grated parmesan for the pesto; salt and pepper.

CROTTIN DE CHAVIGNOL – tiny goat cheeses from Chavignol, a village next to Sancerre. Some cheese merchants keep Chavignols in big jars of olive oil, something English producers have also started doing – it's an idea and taste we like, though make sure the cheeses have not been in the oil too long as they will disintegrate after a while. Chavignol-Sancerre is a close relation, different only in that it has a paler rind, which is a sign that it is less mature. Either will grill well, as indeed will many little softish cheeses, whether they are made with goat, sheep or cow's milk. Buy by eye, a half or whole cheese per head.

OTHER INGREDIENTS – virgin olive oil for frying and for the pesto; fresh white bread to go with the soup and cheese.

WINES – vegetables have their own not inconsiderable levels of acidity even when they taste sweet, which is perhaps the reason why a minestrone, though it contains a little red wine, is not easily matched. However, Marzemino is what Don Giovanni drinks with his last supper in Mozart's opera and is robust enough to stand up to the commotions that ensue. (Pour the wine, he orders Leporello; he tastes, then praises it: "*Eccellente Marzemino!*") Made from the grape of the same name in the mountainous region north-east of Lake Garda, half-way to the ancient city of Trento, Marzemino is a biggish wine, a little bitter when young.

Alternatively, go further north still, beyond Trento, for a not dissimilar and certainly not lesser red – Teroldego Rotaliano, named after it's grape and the *campo rotaliano* where it grows. Adnams currently have a 1983 Teroldego and a 1982 Teroldego Riserva on their list, both by Conti Martini; while a 1983 Marzemino, Conti Bossi Fedrigotti is imported by Ciborio in London; Winecellars and their associated The Market retail chain list Ronco di Mompiano, Pasolini, from the Brescia region, which combines 70% marzemino with 30% merlot, and 1983 Teroldego by Roberto Zeni.

Finally, why not change to white wine after the red – Chavignol is not only a village producing excellent cheese but some of the best Sancerre. Look for a recent vintage, and let the sauvignon grape provide a little extra spice at the end of this meal.

PREPARATION AND PRECOOKING

Cold, though not iced, minestrone is a speciality of Milan, so you could cook yours in the morning or even the night before and chill it; and there are those who insist that a reheated minestrone is better still, though we believe they are wrong. Preparation and cooking slide into each other with this dish, taking no more than 1½ hours in all, except for the dried beans. It's an easy soup, with one simple principle – cook the harder vegetables first, leaving the softest last.

Soak the dried beans in cold water overnight; alternatively pour boiling water over them and they will be ready for cooking in about 2-3 hours.

About 1½ hours in advance, lay out your ingredients, quantities as given in the shopping list or in proportion. Peel and chop the Spanish onion and roughly chop 2 peeled garlic cloves. Roughly chop the bacon rashers if using, and the various herbs, fresh and dried, though not the basil, which is for the pesto later.

In a large casserole heat 4 tablespoons of virgin olive oil, add what you have just chopped, and stir – the garlic must not burn or it will taste bitter, spoiling other flavours too.

After a few minutes, add the canned tomatoes, tomato purée, all the dried vegetables – i.e. the soaked cannellini or borlotti beans, split peas and barley – and the glass of red wine, and cook for 2 minutes on medium heat. Cover with hot water from the kettle so that the vegetables are about ½ inch (1 cm) under its surface, and leave to simmer gently for 30 minutes, lid on. Stir occasionally, adding a little more hot water as necessary.

Meanwhile prepare the remaining ingredients. Wash and scrub the new potatoes and carrots; don't peel either of them but top and tail the carrots. Wash, top and tail the French beans, stringing them if necessary. Pick over the spinach, remove hard stalks, wash the leaves in several changes of water and let them drip dry. Shell the broad beans and peas. Top and tail the courgettes and leeks, checking the latter are free from earth inside the rolled green leaves. Wash the celery.

Break the pasta into short pieces if it's in spaghetti form. Separately chop the celery, carrots, French beans, courgettes and leeks, all into 1 inch (2.5 cm) pieces. Coarsely chop the spinach. If the potatoes are bigger than those described in the shopping list, cut them in half, otherwise leave them whole. Don't add any of these ingredients to the pan just yet, and keep them apart.

When the beans, split peas, barley, tomatoes, etc., have been simmering for 30 minutes, add 1 teaspoon of salt and a little fresh black pepper to the pan, but be careful – salt tends to disappear without trace only to come back later. Test the beans after a further 10 minutes – 40 in all so far; if they are done – soft but still with a little resistance to the bite – add the chopped leeks, carrots and celery to the pan.

5 minutes later add the potatoes – and, after a further 5 minutes, the spinach, French beans and pasta. 5 minutes later again, add the broad beans, peas and courgettes. Pour over a little more hot water if necessary and cook for a final 5 minutes – a real minestrone should be so thick that even a heavy spoon will stand up in it. Because of its considerable mass it will keep hot for quite some time with the lid on; and you can reheat it, of course, provided you stir it a little.

Meanwhile make the pesto. Put the pine nuts in a mortar and pound (pesto derives from *pestare*, to pound). Skin the remaining 2 cloves of garlic, add them to the mortar and pound. Put in the grated parmesan, salt and pepper, and enough virgin olive oil to make a paste. Strip the basil plants, tear the leaves into small bits, and put them in the mortar. Continue to pound and grind until you have a dark green, thick sauce. (You could make the pesto earlier, of course, but it will lose some of its fragrance if it has to wait, so we prefer to prepare it last; you could also use a processor, which saves work and time, but makes rather too smooth a paste for our taste.)

Pick some big leaves – from a vine, or walnut tree, for example – to grill the cheeses in and put the cherries on. Don't pick leaves you don't know enough about or can't identify though – some are toxic.

Take the cheeses out of the refrigerator if still there – they are only small and will warm quickly; wash and dry the leaves for grilling them later.

Wash and pick over the cherries. Line a basket or cover a platter with leaves and put the cherries on top when dry. Keep in a cool place.

COOKING AND PRESENTATION

Serve the minestrone straight from the casserole, with a good dollop of pesto on top of each helping, including seconds. Offer chunks of white bread on the side.

Don't worry if there is a pause between the minestrone and cheese – a big dish can stand a little lingering over.

Preheat the grill to maximum temperature. Oil the grid and lay out a big leaf per crottin. Put the cheeses on top, and cover with another leaf each. Slide under the grill, reduce the heat just a little and watch – the idea is to grill quickly, under high heat, but leaves will react differently according to their hardness and thickness; it does not matter if they char towards the end, but they must not catch fire. Take the grid out after 2-3 minutes and turn the cheeses, complete with their leaves, using a wooden spatula or similar tool. Return to the grill and cook for a little longer, not quite as much as the first time. Serve from the grid on to individual plates, with the Sancerre and washed cherries on the side.

MAINLY FROM THE GARDEN

Don't let the longish shopping list put you off – it's not an expensive one, nor does it mean much work once you have your ingredients at home.

Ricotta, with crudités of tomato, spring onion and new broad beans

Grilled pork chops with courgettes

Summer pudding with cream

A comparison of Pinot Grigio and Pinot Gris

SHOPPING LIST

PORK CHOPS – ask for loin or chump chops from a young animal and have them cut about 1 inch (2.5 cm) thick; 1 chop per person.

RICOTTA – a soft white Italian cheese, not unlike cottage cheese at first sight, but rather smoother in texture and taste. Originally made from the whey left over in the production of other cheeses, it is now usually mixed with whole milk, from cows or sheep, with a fat content of 20-30 percent. Ask if it's really fresh, and buy 3 oz (75 g) per starter. Refrigerate as soon as you get it home.

CREAM – a little cream, whipped or not, would go well with the summer pudding. Allow 1 fl oz (25 ml) double cream per portion.

VEGETABLES FOR THE CRUDITÉS – tomatoes, spring onions and broad beans, all for eating raw accompanied by the ricotta. Buy by eye, depending on what's available and best, also judging quantities that way. At the height of summer you might just find some genuine Mediterranean tomatoes, which, sliced and sprinkled with a little olive oil, black pepper and salt, can be big enough to make a delicious meal by themselves. (They should not need lemon juice or vinegar to heighten their flavour, as they contain enough acidity of their own.) Look out for new broad beans, in bright green pods that have not yet grown to monster size or you may find their contents too hard and no longer sweet enough to eat raw, and serve just with a little salt. Be careful with spring onions as summer advances – the bigger they grow the sharper, and potentially more indigestible, they are likely to become.

SAGE – one of the best herbs to flavour pork with, and easily grown in the garden. Many greengrocers sell it fresh. Count 6 leaves or so per chop.

COURGETTES – buy them small, of even size, so that 3 or 4 make 1 helping.

FRUIT FOR THE SUMMER PUDDING – most kinds of berries will contribute handsomely to this delicious but simply prepared pudding. Our best ever, big enough to serve 6-8, contained 8 oz (250 g) each of strawberries, red currants, black currants and black cherries, plus 4 oz (125 g) raspberries; however, red or white cherries, bilberries, blackberries, wild blueberries, logan-berries, etc., can be excellent substitutes for any or all.

OTHER INGREDIENTS FOR THE SUMMER PUDDING – you will need 1 teaspoon lemon juice; 1 small loaf of white bread, preferably yesterday's because it is easier to cut, but emphatically not a sliced one; a little granulated sugar.

OLIVE OIL – some virgin oil to serve on the side with the first course, and for preparing the chops and courgettes for the grill.

CRÈME DE CASSIS – black currant liqueur – 2 tablespoons would help to concentrate the flavour of the summer pudding. (A small bottle, best kept in the refrigerator because of its relatively low alcoholic strength, is always useful – mix it with dry white wine, about 1 part to 5, for a kir.)

WINES – compare Pinot Grigio from Italy with Pinot Gris (Tokay) from Alsace – begin with a young Italian, such as 1985 Pinot Grigio, Grave del Friuli, Collavini, and finish with a rather older Tokay d'Alsace, Domaine Weinbach, for example.

PREPARATION AND PRECOOKING

Make the summer pudding 2 days in advance if you can, giving it time to settle in the refrigerator; we use a 2½ pint (1.5 litre) pudding basin for the quantities described in the shopping list.

With a sharp knife thinly slice the loaf, about ½ inch (1 cm) thick, but be careful not to break the bread, especially if it is still fresh. Remove crusts from individual slices, and line the basin, beginning at the bottom – you should have enough slices left to cover the top later.

Wash the berries, cherries, etc., and drain well or the water will dilute their flavour. Stem the currants – hold a spray over a bowl, and gently pull it through the prongs of a fork, letting the berries fall into the bowl. Stone the cherries – you'll need a cherry stoner to do this successfully, a simple cheap gadget. Hull the strawberries and, with a small pointed knife, cut around each stem and pull out the fibrous core.

Find an enamelled or stainless steel saucepan big enough to hold all the fruit. Put in the currants first, add a little sugar – say up to 4 oz (125 g) depending on the natural sweetness of the ingredients – 1 teaspoon lemon juice and about ¼ pint (150 ml) water, and stew gently over low heat until the currants begin to dissolve. Add the cherries and turn them over for a few seconds, then add the blackberries, strawberries and raspberries; turn off the heat – the softer the berries, the less heat they should be exposed to. Last, pour in the black currant liqueur, about 2 tablespoons.

Ladle the fruit into the bread-lined pudding basin, reserving most of the juice, and gently pressing down the fruit if necessary.

Finally place the bread slices on top, making a flat, even lid that fits into the ring of bread. Spoon a little juice down the insides of the basin and over the lid, and save the rest in a jug. Cover the basin with cling film and foil, place a small plate on top and some weights – we use 4 lb (2 kg) weights. Refrigerate with the extra juice for 1-2 days.

An hour or so before the first guest is due, take the chops from the refrigerator, put the wines in if not already there, and prepare your charcoal fire if you are going to grill outdoors.

Pour a little olive oil over the chops and rub in. Stick 2 or 3 sage leaves on each side.

Pod the broad beans. Don't panic if you discover only now that they are too hard or bitter to eat raw – put some unsalted water on a high heat, lid on, while you continue podding; when the water is boiling, drop in the beans and cook for 2 minutes, uncovered. Drain through a colander, rinse under cold water to stop further cooking, and set aside to dry.

Wash the spring onions and courgettes; trim their ends and cut the courgettes lengthwise, in halves. Rinse the tomatoes.

Whip the cream for the summer pudding. Use an electric whisk if you have one, but be careful not to overbeat. Put the whipped cream back in the refrigerator.

COOKING AND PRESENTATION

Check the charcoal grill or preheat an electric or gas grill to maximum heat.

Assemble the starters. Portion out the ricotta on individual plates. Slice the tomatoes if big, quarter if small, and put them next to the white cheese for contrast. Add the beans and spring onions, and serve with olive oil, salt and pepper on the side.

Season the chops with salt and pepper and put them on or under the hot grill for 1 minute. Turn, and grill at the same high heat for 1 more minute. Meanwhile brush the courgettes with olive oil and sprinkle with salt and black pepper. Increase the distance of the grid from the fire, or reduce the heat on the electric or gas grill – the pork chops should be cooked through, but must do so slowly or the outsides will burn before they are done.

Put on the courgettes, cut sides to the source of the heat so they will be better sealed. Continue to cook the meat and vegetables for 4 minutes. Turn both, and grill for another 4 minutes at the same moderate heat, making a total of 10 minutes for the chops, 8 for the courgettes.

Take the summer pudding from the refrigerator and turn it out of the basin on to a suitable platter or plate. Cut it at table, like a cake, offering extra juice and whipped cream on the side.

FOR MIDSUMMER DAY

A meal you can prepare the night before, as only the potatoes will need boiling at the last moment. A fish kettle would be useful, but you can easily improvise if necessary.

Asparagus

Poached cold sea trout with mayonnaise; new potatoes

Strawberries with cream

English white wines

SHOPPING LIST

SEA OR SALMON TROUT – for best flavour order a wild rather than farmed specimen if possible, certainly not one that has been frozen. Wild sea trout are in season from March to August, with prices coming down near the level of farmed ones in May or so. You can recognize inferior-tasting farmed sea trout by their duller brownish colour and short nibbled tail fins – they are kept at such close quarters they tend to go for each other when feeding. When you pick up the fish look for shining, slippery skin, bright not sunken eyes, and pink rather than dull red gills as signs of freshness; have it gutted. A fish approximately 20 inches (50 cm) long, about 3 lb (1.5 kg) in weight, is ample for 6 people.

ASPARAGUS – buy it, like all the ingredients for this menu, only the day before the meal if not on the day itself. As described already in Menu 1 (see p. 12), look for freshness – the white ends tell if the asparagus was cut only recently, or if too much moisture has been lost. Check the tips are intact and closed like fresh buds – they snap easily in transport. Reject sticks which are limp and no longer round or firm. It helps both when cooking and portioning out if they are approximately uniform in size and shape. Allow at least 6 good sticks per person, though even double that is not too much. Remember, too, indigenous asparagus has but a short season, and like the rest of this meal is very light. At home, wrap the asparagus in a clean damp cloth and store in the salad tray of your refrigerator unless you can cook it soon.

NEW POTATOES – choose small ones, so that 4 or 5 of similar size amount to no more than a good handful or helping per person.

STRAWBERRIES – buy the freshest domestic strawberries you can find. By all means use your eyes, looking for firmness and colour, but don't forget the taste. Like so much other fruit, strawberries are grown primarily for looks and ease of transport nowadays, as if no one recalled how fragrant they can be. As above, allow generously per person – soon you will have to make do with badly ripened imports again.

LEMONS – to dress the asparagus with, a quarter wedge per person; you will also need some to acidulate the asparagus water – half a lemon for a biggish load – and a tablespoon or so of juice for the mayonnaise; don't buy any to go with the sea trout, though – only very oily or no longer fresh fish benefits from lemon juice.

CREAM – double or whipping cream; 1 fl oz (25 ml) provides 1 modest helping.

EGGS – for the mayonnaise; 2 yolks are easier to start off with than 1, and will make enough for 6 helpings, but be sure you have a couple extra just in case things need to be fixed.

VIRGIN OLIVE OIL – ½ pint (300 ml) makes 4 generous helpings of mayonnaise; but you will also need some for the asparagus, letting your guests pour their own, so don't be caught short.

SUGAR – some caster sugar for the strawberries.

WINES – if everything bar the olive oil is indigenous on your menu, why not have domestic wine? It's surprising how many people in Britain have never even tried English wines. Some are delightful indeed – carefully grown, expertly made but unpretentious, with the kind of scent and fresh taste that many wines, especially white wines, have when drunk in the region in which they are made. Look for Astley Madeleine Angenvin from Worcestershire, Chalkhill Müller-Thurgau from Wiltshire, Wootton Seyval Blanc from Somerset, for example, and get more than one – it's unlikely your guests wouldn't enjoy a little English tasting.

PREPARATION AND PRECOOKING

Cook the fish the night before, or early enough on the day – it ought to cool well before serving. Put the trout on the drainer in the fish kettle. Alternatively, improvise with an oval saucepan or deep baking tin; make a cradle of foil so that you won't break the fish when lifting it out. Punch a few holes in the foil for drainage and place like a lining in the pan, fish on top. Cover but don't drown with cold water, salt well and put on a high heat, lid on. Bring to the boil, boil for 2-3 minutes, then turn off and leave to cool, uncovered – fish cooks at temperatures far below the boiling point of water; it is done as soon as its core reaches 145°F/63°C; there is no point in extended exposure to this temperature, and to raise it would break down the fibres, reducing them to mush.

Tackle the asparagus while the fish is in the water. Once again, there are special cookers with perforated insets which make it possible to part boil, part steam, asparagus. If you have one you most probably know what to do, so here is the basic method. A normal saucepan, deep enough to cover the sticks lying on their sides, is all you need. Put cold water into it, salt, and the juice of half a lemon to prevent the asparagus from going grey. Turn on heat.

Meanwhile wash the asparagus in cold water, being careful not to damage the tips. With a sharp knife cut off the dry bottom ends. If you have the time or inclination, you can peel away the hard outer skin: hold the stick, tip towards you; begin lengthwise, with a small paring knife, finding the thickness of hard outer fibre at the bottom first; carefully guide the blade along the stalk and towards you, until the skin thins out, ending with the deepening green of the stick. Peeling is recommended by many cooks, but, quite apart from the work involved, has its drawbacks – if, as most afficionados of this vegetable do, you eat the sticks by hand, they can easily turn out too limp to be held comfortably; unless the asparagus turns out tough after all, in which case you probably should have rejected it in the first place, you can suck the soft flesh from the hard outer fibres at the bottom of the stick – a little less elegant perhaps, but still tasty, and so much easier to do.

Drop the prepared sticks into boiling water, thick ends first. Let the water come back to the boil for a few seconds only. Reduce to a barely noticeable simmer. With a perforated drainer or skimmer lift out a stick after 5 minutes if it is thin; 12 minutes should be enough for all but the very thickest. Test by bite – tip, middle, bottom. Take out quickly, spreading the sticks on a clean cloth or double layer of kitchen paper. Lay on a plate when cool, preferably the one you will be serving from. Cover loosely and store in a cool place, in the refrigerator if necessary.

Make the mayonnaise. There are two methods: one mechanical, the other by hand, taking but a few minutes longer. There is a reward for the extra work, though – whatever the makers of food processors or blenders may claim, hand-beaten mayonnaise has a fuller taste and texture, noticeable especially with good oil. Here is the slightly harder method then.

First, measure out your oil – say ½ pint (300 ml) for 4 generous helpings – into a jug with a good pouring lip. Next, make sure the oil is more or less at room temperature – you can warm it by standing the jug in warm water if necessary. Separate the yolks from 2 eggs and drop into a mixing bowl of medium size. Add a three-finger pinch of salt, double that of mustard powder, freshly ground black pepper, and a teaspoon of lemon juice. Stir with a wooden spoon or whisk, either of good weight, until the mixture is quite smooth and no longer cold if the eggs came from the refrigerator – they may refuse to mix with the oil, i.e. curdle, if their temperature is too low.

Add a few drops of the oil. Stir round and round at a steady speed. When the sauce turns shiny, add a little more oil. Continue to beat in the same fashion, gradually increasing the trickle of oil to a thin flow. Keep your eye on the mayonnaise – if it loses the glistening shine, stop pouring oil but stir a little harder until it is quite smooth again. If it grows too stiff, add a little more lemon juice, and see how the colour suddenly pales. In the end you should have a rich, glistening sauce, stiff enough to stand the spoon or whisk in it. Let the mayonnaise sit for a while before attempting to correct the taste – the mustard powder at least takes a few minutes to develop its flavour.

Don't panic if your sauce curdles. It's easier to repair it than make a new mayonnaise. Break a new yolk into a fresh bowl. Don't add anything – just stir, until it's smooth and at room temperature. Add ½ teaspoon of the curdled mayonnaise. Beat until they blend. When this new mix is quite shiny, add a little more of the curdled mayonnaise at a time, until you have used up the lot. Don't forget the rest of the oil if there is any left. Last, put the mayonnaise in the bowl you will serve it from. Store in the refrigerator, where it will keep for a day if there is any left over at the end of the meal.

If you need a larger quantity of mayonnaise, start off with 3 yolks – the more the easier – and increase the volume of oil roughly in proportion. There are several reasons why quantities are flexible and, ultimately, have to be judged as you go along when making mayonnaise – the size of the yolks, the consistency of the oil and the desired density of the sauce itself, most importantly.

Lift the fish from the water when you can comfortably put your hand in it. Let the fish dry and cool a little further. Some cooks, traditionalists especially, skin a sea trout at this stage, but we don't – the fish stays moister this way. Put it in the refrigerator, loosely covered with foil.

Only a few things remain to be done – an hour or so before your first guest is due to arrive, take the fish and asparagus from the refrigerator – they should be cool but not icy when served. Make sure your wines are getting cold.

Rinse the strawberries in cold water – quickly, without undue pressure. If you really have the time and feel so inclined, cut round the stems and leaves with a small pointed knife to remove the hulls from the fruit; if you don't, no one really minds pulling the leaves and stalks from good strawberries on their plate. Cover with a cloth and leave in a cool place.

If you want to whip it, pour the double cream into a generous mixing bowl. Beat it with an electric or wire whisk, but be careful with the former not to overbeat. Put the whipped cream into the bowl you will be serving it from. Return to the refrigerator.

Scrub the new potatoes with a brush until quite clean, so that they need not be peeled when done, and set aside.

COOKING AND PRESENTATION

Really small potatoes will take no more than about 10 minutes to cook from immersion in boiling salt water, which you might start to preheat when the first guests are about to arrive.

Drop the potatoes into the fast boiling water as you are ready to sit down to the first course. Let the water come back to the boil, then reduce it a little, so that the potatoes will not get damaged by its movement.

Offer the asparagus with virgin olive oil, lemon wedges, salt and fresh black pepper. Let your guests make their own dressings.

Present the fish on its plate. With a small knife, cut through the skin along the line of the backbone. Gradually work down to the bone itself. Ease the top fillet from the bone first. Serve a mixture of top and bottom fillets to each guest. When all the flesh is removed from the first side, lift the backbone by the tail fin and pull away, up to and including the head. Serve the second side in the same way as the first. Offer the fish, potatoes and mayonnaise at the same time.

Present the strawberries, cream and caster sugar in separate bowls.

LIGHT BUT ELEGANT

A slight menu, for when it's hot or appetites
are not expected to be great.

*Lamb's lettuce salad, with hazelnut and lemon
dressing*

Roast quail; mange-touts in butter

Petits suisses; fresh figs

Muscat d'Alsace

SHOPPING LIST

QUAIL – most of these small game birds are raised commercially
nowadays and are available all year round, generally of con-
sistent quality, but avoid frozen ones if you can. Ask for them
dressed and barded with pork fat, ready for the oven; you may
need 2 birds per person if they are tiny.

MANGE-TOUTS – or snow-peas, abundant nonetheless in early
summer. Look for smallish, flat pods, that snap rather than bend
in your fingers. They will look less once topped and tailed, and
shrink when cooked, so allow 2 good handfuls per portion.

LAMB'S LETTUCE – small, pale green leaves, which ought to be no
more than dewy if not dry. No lighter salad is to be found in our
markets, so, as above, count at least 2 handfuls per starter, or 2
oz (50 g).

LEMON – half a fruit to acidulate the water for the mange-touts; plus another half to dress lamb's lettuce for 6.

ORANGE – 1 fruit will dress enough figs for 6.

FRESH FIGS – green or purple, either kind is delicious if ripe, but reject oozing or bruised fruit. Sizes vary considerably, though be suspicious of figs that are small – they can be quite dry inside seemingly perfect skins. Count 2 per person.

PETITS SUISSES – tiny tots of *double creme* from France, called thus because of the young Swiss cowherd who first suggested that a little fresh cream be added to the curds of a local cheese, or so the story goes. Look carefully at what is on offer – are the shapes still firm, surfaces moist and perfectly white? Buy according to size, 2 or more per head. Store in the refrigerator.

BUTTER – you need rather less than 1 oz (25 g) to coat each helping of mange-touts, fresh and unsalted if you can.

HAZELNUT OIL – a light golden oil, with a distinct hazelnut flavour that will lift all tender greens. Buy only a little container, a first pressing from the most recent harvest if possible, and keep it in the refrigerator.

WINE – Muscat d'Alsace is dry, greenish when young, but quite unrelated to Muscadet. This intensely grapey white could easily take you right through this simple meal, starting with a recent and finishing with an older vintage if you like, as these wines mature very well. Hugel, easily recognized by the distinctive yellow labels, is an obvious name to look for, but there are Beyer, Blanck, Heydt, Trimbach and others too, for standards are high in this eastern-most region of France.

PREPARATION AND PRECOOKING

An hour or so in advance take the quail from the refrigerator, and put your wine in if necessary. Lightly butter a roasting tin.

Put in the birds, barded side up, sprinkle with a little salt and set aside to warm up.

Wash, top and tail the mange-touts, pulling away any strings, and discarding limp pods. Meanwhile bring some salt water to the boil, lid on; squeeze in the juice of half a lemon when boiling fast, and drop in the mange-tout. Cook, lid off, for 3 minutes. Drain through a colander, cool with cold running water and set aside.

Sort through the lamb's lettuce, discarding long stems or roots. Wash gently in plenty of cold water, drain and dry with a salad centrifuge or by swinging in a clean tea cloth. Set aside in a cool place.

Gently rinse the figs and pat dry with kitchen paper. With a sharp knife trim the remaining stems and quarter each fig downwards, but take care not to squash the fruit if your knife is not razor sharp, producing unsightly cuts. Arrange the segments in a bowl, squeeze the orange, strain, and pour the juice over the figs. Set aside and occasionally spoon the orange juice back over the figs – they will need a while to develop their full flavour.

COOKING AND PRESENTATION

As your starter is very light, plan to follow up with the main course with minimum delay. Before you sit down to the first course, preheat the oven to gas 8/450°F/230°C. Put the quail in the preheated oven and they should be done in 20 minutes.

Dress the lamb's lettuce at table. Pour over the hazelnut oil first. Sprinkle on a little salt, fresh black pepper and lemon juice, and toss until all leaves appear evenly coated.

With the quail still in the oven, melt a good knob of butter in a frying pan over highish heat. When the butter is golden brown, add the mange-touts, stir and keep stirring for 3-4 minutes, adding a little salt and fresh black pepper as they are cooking. Turn them into a bowl, and serve on separate vegetable plates.

Take the quail from the oven, remove the remains of barding fat and strings, set on individual plates and take to the table immediately.

Offer the petits suisses on a pretty plate or platter, direct from the refrigerator, together with the figs.

CHEESE AND SALAD FROM THE SOUTH OF FRANCE

This menu is simple and quickly prepared, especially if you have a big bowl to make and present the salad in. What's in a real salade Niçoise though? Even the locals themselves seem unable to agree, perhaps because they, too, depend on what they will find and fancy in the market on the day.

Salade Niçoise

Roquefort

Peaches

Pernod, Ricard, or a white wine from Provence
with the salad
Muscat de Frontignan with the cheese and peaches

SHOPPING LIST

TOMATOES – big bulging Mediterranean ones would be best, 1 per head unless really large; alternatively choose firm salad tomatoes, perhaps 3 per portion.

GREEN OR YELLOW PEPPERS – the latter provides extra colour and flavour, but green will do handsomely; sizes vary, of course – even half a pepper can be plenty for 1 helping.

HARICOTS VERTS – a handful per portion.

BROAD BEANS – young ones, which can be eaten just as they come, would be best, but you can soften more mature broad beans by cooking them in water for a couple of minutes or so. Pods are deceptive – even big ones can be empty – so allow 2 big handfuls per head, or 1 lb (500 g) for 2.

BASIL – 4 leaves per portion.

LEMON – 1 to acidulate the water for the haricots and broad beans if necessary.

PEACHES – big purple and yellow peaches would be best, 1 per person; inspect their skins – are they intact, showing neither bruises nor other signs of too much softness?

ARTICHOKE HEARTS – buy them *sotto olio* – marinated in oil, not vinegar or brine. Count 2 or 3 per helping.

OLIVES – the tiny, unstoned black ones with a deep glossy shine that grow around Nice usually find their way into this kind of salad.

CAPERS – allow about ½ oz (15 g) per portion.

ANCHOVIES – count 2 fillets per head.

TUNA – a small 3 oz (75 g) can in olive oil will make 2 portions.

EGGS – are easier to peel when boiled a few days old, but you will have to get them home to find out – the older the egg, the bigger the air pocket it contains, which means that a fresh egg won't rattle if you shake it next to your ear, and it will sink to the bottom when put into water. Store eggs in the refrigerator, away from strong foodstuffs – they have pores through which they can take in all sorts of flavours and smells. Size 1 or 2; 1 egg per head.

OLIVE OIL – a first cold pressing from Provence or Tuscany to dress the salad, just enough to coat the ingredients.

ROQUEFORT – without doubt one of the pinnacles in the art of cheesemaking, produced at Roquefort-sur-Soulzon with sheep's milk brought from all over the surrounding regions. Shaped into cylinders approximately 1 foot (30 cm) across, the cheeses finally mature in the humid and naturally ventilated limestone caves of the Combalou. They are salted individually in the process – unfortunately with extra doses for cheeses that will have to travel far. Insist on a taste before you lay out a lot of money just for the name, for some are hopelessly oversalted.

WINES – many salads don't get on with wine, primarily because of the acidity inherent in many raw vegetables as well as in most dressings. Although neither vinegar nor lemon are used in this recipe, anchovies, tuna and eggs all pose their own problems, so a pastis like Pernod or Ricard with plenty of water and ice might serve not only as an aperitif but take you through the first course entirely. Not everyone likes aniseed flavour though, and so you could offer a Provençal white instead – Bellet and Château de Cremat from the hills behind Nice; Château Simone, blanc de blancs, from the tiny appellation Palette next door to Aix; or a Cassis, Domaine du Paternel, for example.

Sauternes is the wine usually mentioned in combination with roquefort – sweet versus sharp – for few wines will stand up to the flavour of this blue cheese, or so the argument goes. We tried the combination, with port, madeira and a number of sweet muscats as well, such as nearby Frontignan and Mireval from the south of France, and have finally come to the conclusion that, for us, none of them work. But draw your own, and get your guests to join in the judgement at the end of this meal.

PREPARATION, COOKING AND PRESENTATION

Most salads should be made more or less at the last possible moment, and *Niçoise* is an exception only in as much as it needs a little extra care in assembly; there are modern cooks who like to refrigerate it before serving, but we don't. Only the eggs and haricots and perhaps the broad beans need to be cooked, though there are traditionalists who say a real *Niçoise* must not contain anything cooked at all.

Begin with the eggs. Put them in a saucepan, cover with cold water and place on medium heat. Time them from the moment bubbles begin to rise; reduce the heat to a simmer for 10 minutes. Plunge them into cold water when they are done – not only will they stop cooking this way, but they will be easier to shell once they have cooled completely.

Meanwhile pod the broad beans. Taste one or two. Unless they are sweet and buttery they will need blanching in boiling water, but you can add them to the boiling haricots for the last 2 minutes of their time, saving yourself the effort of preparing a separate saucepan.

Fill another saucepan, big enough to take the haricots and broad beans if necessary, with salt water, and set to boil over high heat, lid on. Continue podding the beans; wash, top and tail the haricots. When the water is boiling fast, squeeze in half a lemon, wait for the froth to die down, and plunge in the haricots only, lid off from now on. Let the water come back to the boil for a few seconds, then reduce it to a simmer. Add the broad beans after 4 minutes if necessary, increase the heat slightly and continue to cook for another 2, making a total of 6 minutes for the haricots. Drain through a colander, immediately rinse with running cold water to prevent further cooking, and set aside to cool.

Wash the peppers in cold water and let drip dry. With a sharp knife cut them into rings, discarding seeds inside, and place in the salad bowl. Add the broad beans and haricots – it does not matter if they are still warm. Add half of the black olives. Sprinkle everything with olive oil, fresh pepper but no salt – put in the anchovy fillets, cut in halves if long, instead. Toss until everything is evenly coated.

Wash the tomatoes and dry. Slice them if big, otherwise quarter.

Sprinkle them with olive oil, a little salt, black pepper, and slide in among the things already in the salad bowl – partly over, partly under – but without further tossing.

Add the artichokes to the salad bowl, distributing them all over.

Take the tuna from the refrigerator. Open the can or cans, pour off the oil, and break up the flesh into bite-size chunks on a separate plate. Add to the salad bowl, like the artichoke hearts before.

Gently crack the shells of the hard-boiled eggs, tapping them with a spoon until they are crazed all over. Peel the eggs and try to pull away the thin membranes inside the shells, but avoid damage to the whites. Quarter the eggs and distribute on top of the salad. Last, scatter the remaining black olives, the capers and basil over the assembly and serve soon, but take the roquefort from the refrigerator first.

Offer the roquefort, pudding wine and peaches at the same time. Arrange the cheese and peaches on big green leaves if you like – from a vine, walnut or chestnut, for example.

AIOLI

A classic Friday dish from Provence, ideal for
big parties and popular with children, too – a
big bowl of gutsy garlic mayonnaise,
traditionally offered with salt cod, snails,
hard-boiled eggs and all sorts of cooked and
raw vegetables.

Aioli

Black currant sorbet

A dry pink wine from Provence

SHOPPING LIST

MANY THINGS, RAW OR COOKED, COME WITH AN AIOLI – even cold
meats, in which case the Provençaux elevate it to the status of a
grand aioli. Here is a list of what we might buy for a party of 6,
though where possible individual portions are also given –
delete or improve on it as you please, but make sure that your
crudités are as crisp as possible.

COD – dried salt cod from Scandinavia, Iceland or North
America is in fact a traditional ingredient along the Mediterranean, where the fish does not occur; it's an acquired taste,
though, and more laborious to prepare than fresh cod, which is
what we use. Count 1 slice per head, about 1 inch (2.5 cm) thick,
from the middle of a biggish fish, but buy and cook your total in
one piece on the day you serve it. Order what you need in
advance if your party is going to be big.

PRAWNS IN THEIR SHELLS – allow 4 oz (125 g) per head, but be guided by your nose if the weather is or has just been very hot; leave the prawns out if they smell at all high; in any case buy them only if you can eat them on the same day.

EGGS – 1 per head, hard-boiled; plus whatever you will need to make the garlic-based mayonnaise – the aioli – which is the heart of the meal. 2 yolks can be stretched to make enough sauce for up to 6, but 3 yolks will render it not only richer but easier to make too. Get some extra eggs in case any break when boiling or shelling, and as a stand-by in case of accidents when making the mayonnaise.

OLIVE OIL – extra virgin, from the first cold pressing, French or Italian, is what you need here, but don't pay through the nose for a pretty bottle – even supermarkets offer the real article nowadays, at reasonable prices; ¾ pint (450 ml) makes plenty of aioli for 6.

GARLIC – fresh summer garlic, without green tips or cores. Count 2 good cloves per head.

WAX BEANS – the yellow variety, a handful each.

CARROTS – 2 smallish ones each.

NEW POTATOES – a good handful, about 4 or 5, each.

LEMON – half a fruit will flavour enough aioli for 6.

TOMATOES – 2 per head, unless you can find the preferable big Mediterranean variety.

CUCUMBER – 1 large fruit will serve 6.

SWEET PEPPERS – green, yellow and red; one of each, if available, to be shared between 6.

CELERY – a head, counting 1 stalk or so per portion.

BUTTON MUSHROOMS – 4 each.

POSSIBLE SUBSTITUTES FOR THE VEGETABLES – artichokes; cauliflower; small courgettes; broad, French and runner beans; fennel bulbs.

BLACK CURRANT SORBET – easily and quickly made, so unless you decide to buy a proprietary make, you will need per helping 4 oz (125 g) black currants, 1 tablespoon sugar and 1 tablespoon each of fresh lime and orange juice. You can substitute lemon for the lime if necessary.

WINE – rosé is the prescribed colour to accompany an aioli, and why not, especially as the south of France abounds with it. Look for Castel Roubine, Côtes de Provence; Château Val Joanis, Côtes du Luberon; Château de Fonscolombe, Côteaux d'Aix-en-Provence; Rosé de Syrah, Domaine du Bosc, vin de pays de l'Herault, for example.

PREPARATION AND PRECOOKING

Make the sorbet a day or more in advance. Quickly rinse the currants under cold water and stem, pulling the sprigs through the prongs of a fork. Put the currants in a saucepan with the sugar, lime and orange juice. Simmer on low heat for about 5 minutes, until the currants are beginning to look a little soft. Blend them in a processor or pass through a sieve, pour into a plastic container and put into the freezer or freezing compartment of your refrigerator. Stir with a fork after 2 hours or so, especially along the edges, to break up the ice. Repeat once more, after another hour or so.

Everything else is best made just before the meal, with crudités left whole as late as possible, ending with the few components that are served hot – the cod and the potatoes, though you could serve the fish cold if you like. Try to present everything as appetizingly as possible, arranged on platters and plates, carefully cut, chopped or sliced, letting the various colours work for you – in other words, give yourself enough time if your party is a big one, and sharpen your knives well.

COOKING AND PRESENTATION

First of all, make sure the oil and eggs for the aioli itself are at room temperature. If not, measure and count out now what you will need, and let it all stand in a warmish place. The cod, too, should be approaching room temperature by the time you poach it; on the other hand, put the wine in the refrigerator if it's not there already.

Hard-boil the eggs next. Put in a pan, cover with cold water and place on medium heat. Reduce to a simmer when you see bubbles rise, and set the timer for 10 minutes. Plunge the boiled eggs into cold water – this stops them cooking further, and makes them easier to shell when cool.

Meanwhile top and tail the wax beans, pulling away strings if any. Rinse and drop them into fast-boiling, slightly salt water for 6 minutes, when they should still be a little crunchy. Drain through a colander, cold rinse, and set aside to cool.

Scrub the carrots and potatoes in cold water with a hard brush, but leave skins intact as far as possible. Prepare a saucepan of salt water to cook the potatoes in later, but don't immerse them now.

Wash the remaining vegetables and let them dry.

Make the aioli itself. Use a mortar and pestle if you have one big enough, otherwise use a heavy mixing bowl and a wooden spoon or wire whisk.

Peel the garlic cloves and pound with the pestle until you have a smooth paste. Alternatively, the broad side of a knife blade, or a garlic press will do – it doesn't matter if the paste is not absolutely smooth.

Separate the egg yolks from their whites into the mortar or bowl, and add the garlic, a little salt, black pepper and lemon juice, about ½ tablespoon for 2-3 yolks. Beat until creamy and smooth. Pour in a few drops – literally – of the olive oil and beat until they have been absorbed into the mix. Pour in a little more oil and continue patiently, adding oil only when the previous quantity has been absorbed. Watch the sauce acquire a shiny, deeply glistening surface. Increase the amounts of oil you pour as the volume of sauce in the bowl grows. Beat faster and harder if you pour too much, until the deep gleam returns. Correct the flavour with a little more salt, pepper and ½ tablespoon lemon juice, but give the sauce time to develop its flavour. It should be very thick at the end – stiff enough to hold a heavy pestle.

Don't worry if the sauce curdles. Break a fresh yolk into a clean mixing bowl, stir until creamy and add a teaspoon of the curdled mix. Beat until you a have a little of the glistening sauce described. Little by little use up the curdled sauce, adding the remaining oil at the end if necessary.

Shell the hard-boiled eggs, being careful not to break their surfaces. Leave them whole and arrange either with the vegetables or on a separate plate. Quarter the tomatoes. Cut the cucumber, celery and carrots into sticks, cut the peppers into rings, trim the mushrooms, and arrange all with the cooked beans, contrasting the various colours of the vegetables and dishes you may have.

Unless you serve it in the mortar you made it in, put the aioli into a suitable plate or soup dish, where its colour can be seen to advantage.

Place the cod in a saucepan or fish kettle, cover with water and a good deal of salt (think of sea water) and set over medium to high heat, depending on the volume, lid on. Be careful not to let the water come to the boil – it should shiver, not roll. A single large piece of the kind described, with the backbone still at its centre, will take about 7 minutes per pound (500 g) to cook; one or more slices, which the heat can penetrate individually, will take approximately 8 minutes from the moment the water begins to stir. Lift the fish from the water when you think it is done, remove the skin, and remove a piece of flesh from the backbone – it should be opaque and come off in big flakes, which is the way to serve it with this meal. Return the fish to the water for a little longer if necessary. Pile the flakes on a big plate and serve hot or cold.

Drop the new potatoes into fast boiling water and test after 12 minutes. Drain when they are done and bring to table in their own bowl.

Meanwhile shell the prawns and arrange them on a separate plate.

Last, don't forget the sorbet. If you made it yourself, take it from the freezer before you sit down to the meal. Otherwise follow the manufacturer's instructions.

COOL BUT NOT WITHOUT SUBSTANCE

A cold meal, rustic but elegant. A blender or processor is necessary for making the cold soup.

Gazpacho

Cold fillet of beef, with fresh horseradish folded in cream; salad of new runner beans

Berries of the season

Rioja – white and red

SHOPPING LIST

GAZPACHO – a cold soup from Spain, which, presented with chunks of brown bread, extra vegetables and hard-boiled eggs on the side, can make a not inconsiderable meal in itself. Here are the ingredients for 6 helpings of our lighter, though slightly luxurious, version, intended only as a starter.

For 6 helpings you will need 1 clove of summer garlic; 6 large ripe tomatoes; 1 large green pepper, which ought to be crisp and without trace of wrinkles; 1 Spanish onion; 1 large cucumber; ¾ pint (450 ml) tomato juice; 2 ripe avocados, preferably of the wrinkly dark kind; 4 tablespoons olive oil; 2 tablespoons red wine vinegar; 1 tablespoon lemon juice; a sprig of coriander.

FRESH HORSERADISH – to go with the beef, one whole or part of a biggish root.

RUNNER BEANS – for the salad; 2 handfuls per head.

BERRIES – whatever is new and strikes your fancy – loganberries are often underrated, but excellent to eat raw when ripe, ditto yellow gooseberries, and, best of all to our tastes, wild blueberries if you can find them.

LEMONS – 1-2 to acidulate the bean water, dress the beans and also the berries.

FILLET OF BEEF – occasionally you can find this prime of prime cuts already cooked in a good delicatessen, but make sure it's still moist and has not been dried out by refrigeration. Buy it in a piece; imagine the slices – between ⅛ and ¼ inch (3-6 mm) thick – that you will need to cover the better part of a dining plate, and you have the size of a portion, but carve the meat yourself, just before serving. Alternatively, order it from your butcher; a whole well hung fillet, which ought to be dark rather than bright red, is the most elegant solution, but sections from the middle fillet, for more even cooking, are just as acceptable of course.

CREAM – a ¼ pint (150 ml) pot will dress enough horseradish for 6.

OLIVE OIL – you will need some for dressing the beans, and for brushing the meat tin.

SUGAR – a little caster sugar for dressing the berries.

WINE – Jerez excepted, Rioja's three wine-making regions (Alta, Alavesa, Baja) are probably Spain's most famous, capable of producing whites and reds of outstanding quality. *Denominaciones de origen* were introduced at the beginning of the seventies, and nowadays a genuine Rioja sports two labels – one in front, giving the usual details, and one on the back, confirming origin and age. Thus a vino de crianza must have spent at least one year in oak cask, plus another in bottle before it can be sold; a reserva would probably have spent three years in oak, and a gran reserva five or more – probably because self-imposed practice by the better producers usually exceeds the minima laid down in the official regulations. Oak, or rather its flavour, is thus the hallmark of Rioja even with white wines, unless you choose one of the modern and very fresh varieties marketed recently. However, maturing in oak alone does not make a great wine, and too much of it can destroy even a good one. Not a few of our tasting notes mention huge noses, little meat and an increasingly salt tail developing an hour from opening or so. What to buy then? Try white, especially the new style, and red from any of the following top bodegas – La Rioja Alta; CUNE (Compania Vinicola del Norte de Espana); Marques de Caceres; R Lopez de Heredia.

PREPARATION AND PRECOOKING

Make the gazpacho in two steps in order to get it cold and to preserve a maximum of crispness for the vegetables – quantities as given in the shopping list or in proportion.

Blend the peeled garlic and 4 of the tomatoes; add half of the green pepper, onion and peeled cucumber, all of them roughly sliced, and blend again. Strain the mixture into a bowl – don't worry about the greyish colour, it gets better later! – and put in your refrigerator. Also chill the tomato juice, if not there already, and the remaining green pepper, onion and cucumber.

Unless you have bought it cooked already, roast the fillet of beef so that it will be cold – slightly refrigerated but not icy – by the time you bring it to table. First, let the meat warm to room temperature, but don't oil or salt it at any time with this recipe. Slightly oil a roasting tin and put to preheat in the oven at gas 9/475°F/240°C. When the oven is hot, quickly place the fillet in the tin and roast at the same very hot temperature for 7 minutes per pound (500 g) for rare, 10 minutes per pound (500 g) for medium meat – the idea is to sear and seal the surfaces as quickly as possible, leaving the meat juicy and pink inside. (In other words, don't choose this dish if you like your beef cooked through, as it wouldn't work with cold fillet.) When the meat is done, let it cool in a warm place, and put in the refrigerator, loosely covered with foil.

Wash the runner beans, top and tail, pulling away strings if any, while you heat enough salt water to boil them in, lid on. Squeeze half a lemon into the fast boiling water, drop in the beans, adjust to a simmer and cook for 6 minutes, uncovered. Drain through a colander and let dry. When the beans have cooled, chop them into pieces about 2 inches (5 cm) long, put in a serving bowl, and set aside ready to be dressed with lemon juice, olive oil, pepper and salt later, when finishing the gazpacho.

About half an hour before serving, roughly chop the remaining vegetables – 2 tomatoes, remaining half of green pepper, onion and cucumber, 2 avocados – and set aside for a moment. Add the tomato juice, olive oil, red wine vinegar, lemon juice, salt and fresh black pepper to the already refrigerated gazpacho mixture and stir well. Put in the chopped vegetables and return the finished soup to the refrigerator. Finely chop the coriander and have it ready to serve on the side – it's an acquired flavour not everyone likes.

Toss the runner beans with olive oil until they all glisten evenly, sprinkle on a little lemon juice, salt and black pepper, and set aside.

Last, whip the cream; wash and grate the horseradish – about 1 tablespoon per portion – and fold into the whipped cream. Set the mix aside in a cool place, as it will take a little while to develop its full flavour.

PRESENTATION

Serve the gazpacho in individual plates, straight from the refrigerator, offering the coriander on the side.

Slice the beef – ⅛ to ¼ inch (3-6 mm) thick – and arrange on a platter or big plate. Offer the horseradish cream piled on a separate plate. Serve the beans on the side with the beef.

Offer the berries last, with a little lemon juice and caster sugar on the side.

SEA BASS BAKED IN SALT

A bafflingly simple method of cooking sea fish, which we learned from a Milanese restaurateur, and found again, for a different fish, in Michel Guérard's revolutionary *Cuisine Gourmande* (Macmillan, 1978). You will need an ovenproof dish big enough to take your fish, but you can improvise with several layers of kitchen foil.

Prosciutto di San Daniele; fresh figs

Sea bass baked in salt; yellow, red and green peppers

Endive, oak leaf and sorrel salad

Fontina d'Aosta

White and red wines from Aosta – Blanc de la Salle, Enfer d'Arvier

SHOPPING LIST

PROSCIUTTO DI SAN DANIELE – rated as highly as Parma, with a slightly meatier flavour perhaps, this ham comes from a small town in north-east Italy, half-way in the narrow strip of land between the Adriatic and the Austrian Alps. Have the ham sliced by machine, as thinly as possible, with sheets of greaseproof paper between the layers or they will be difficult to separate without tearing. Watch as the slices come off the piece, and judge how many you will need per head – 2 or 3 should be enough. Keep the ham wrapped and store in the refrigerator; be careful not to put anything on top.

FONTINA D'AOSTA – "a cheesemaker's dream come true", or so Vivienne Marquis and Patricia Haskell describe this Italian classic from French-speaking Aosta (*The Cheese Book*, Leslie Frewin, 1966), rating it among the top dozen cheeses made anywhere today. It combines the qualities of emmenthal, gruyère and port salut, they say, but judge for yourself. Fontina travels well enough, so you should have no problem finding it in good condition. Buy it by eye, allowing a good piece per head if you want to concentrate on it alone, as it might well deserve; alternatively get one or two of the cheeses above to compare the fontina to and put them, yourself and your friends to the test.

SEA BASS – a predatory fish prized as one of the finest in the Mediterranean, yet quite at home in our waters too, especially in summer, when it can also be found in estuaries and the lower reaches of rivers. Ask the fishmonger in advance what your chances are of obtaining what you will need – a young specimen weighing just over 1 lb (500 g) will just serve 2 people; one of 3 lb (1.5 kg) more generously 4; but sea bass can grow much bigger – the British rod-caught record stands at more than 18 lb – and the size of your oven may limit you, as we found with a three-pounder that was about as long as our standard oven would take, though you could of course bake more than one fish at a time. Have the bass gutted through the gills so that no salt will get into the body cavity, but not scaled; cook it on the day you get it – it would be a pity to reduce the lovely freshness of its flavour.

FIGS – buy green or purple ones, even a mix for this colourful meal, 1 or 2 per head depending on size and how much ham you will put on each plate. Look carefully, though, especially late in summer – figs can ripen as early as June in central Italy, for example, and bruise only too easily in transport. Store them in the refrigerator if they appear to be going over the top, loosely covered with a damp cloth to prevent drying out.

SWEET PEPPERS – yellow, red and green, the more colours the merrier. Get 1 biggish pepper per portion.

ENDIVE, OAK LEAF AND SORREL – first of all look around at what there is on offer, and adjust your plans according to freshness and quality if necessary. Cool, crisply curly heads with a bit of weight and heart are what you ought to find as regards the first two, while a few handfuls of individual long-stemmed sorrel leaves would provide a little spice.

HERBS – a little fresh thyme and marjoram for the fish.

LEMON – a little lemon juice to dress the salad with.

VIRGIN OLIVE OIL – a few tablespoons for cooking the peppers, as well as for the salad dressing.

SALT – coarse sea salt is what you need, and plenty of it, for the fish will have to be completely encased in it. 3 lb (1.5 kg) will cover a specimen for 2 servings as described, but a bigger one obviously needs more. Salt is always useful though, and inexpensive, so err on the generous side – only when burying your fish in it will you know exactly how much salt it takes.

WINE – before you search and search, but still can't find Blanc de la Salle or Enfer d'Arvier, we ought to confess we have drunk and liked them, but in Aosta itself, with a little fontina on the side. However, only a little further down the valley grow red Donnaz and Carema, the latter just over the provincial border in Piedmonte. Your choice then widens as you go south, with white Erbaluce di Caluso and red Rubino di Cantavenna, made with the barbera grape, just to begin with.

PREPARATION AND PRECOOKING

An hour before dinner take the fish and the other ingredients – prosciutto and figs excepted – from the refrigerator, but put the white wine in unless it's there already.

Wash the peppers and dry them. Cut them in half lengthwise with a sharp knife, and remove the stems, opaque white membranes and seeds. Cut into long strips, ⅙ to ¼ inch (4-6 mm) wide, mix the colours, if various, and set aside.

Remove coarse outer leaves from the salad heads and discard. Cut off the roots, unfold the leaves and decide whether they need washing – if a head was well closed up, it may be quite clean inside. Wash in cold water if necessary, drying the leaves in a salad centrifuge or swinging them overhead in a clean dish cloth. Pick over the sorrel leaves, cutting long stems, and set aside with the rest in a cool place.

Take the figs and prosciutto from the refrigerator. Rinse the figs and dab dry with kitchen paper. Making sure your knife is razor sharp, first cut off any dry bits from the very top of the figs, then set each fruit on its bottom and quarter from the top, with a cutting, not squashing motion. Arrange the figs and prosciutto on a flat plate – the shapes and colours show up particularly well on plain white.

Unwrap the prosciutto and lay out on plates, just slightly overlapping.

Deal with the fish last, to give it time to warm up a little, and to avoid transferring its smell to other things you handle in preparation. Be careful not to hurt yourself – sea bass sport vicious spiny rays in their fins, which you might cut off with kitchen scissors now, first of all. Next find a dish, which must be ovenproof and just deep enough to let you bury the fish in it. Alternatively, on a baking sheet, shape a suitable container from layers of aluminium foil – it can be quite tight at the sides, leaving no more than 2 inches (5 cm) around the fish, and it need not be too deep either, for sea salt is coarse enough to let you heap it over the top.

Cover the bottom of the dish or similar container with 1 inch (2.5 cm) salt, put in your fish and pour more salt over and around it until the top layer, too, is 1 inch (2.5 cm) deep, and the bass buried.

Work out the timetable – smallish fish up to 3 lb (1.5 kg), started at room temperature, will need 30 minutes in a preheated hot oven – gas 7/425°F/220°C; for a bigger specimen calculate approximately 15 minutes per pound (500 g) at the same temperature. Don't forget to allow enough time for preheating the oven.

COOKING AND PRESENTATION

With the fish well on its way in the oven, serve the ham and figs.

Prepare to cook the peppers when the fish is nearly done, or better still, if there are two cooks available have one serve the sea bass while the other finishes the peppers. They will only need a few minutes and should be served piping hot, from the frying pan more or less.

Take a frying pan big enough to take all the cut peppers without piling them in, 1 inch (2.5 cm) deep at most, but don't put them in yet; just cover the bottom of the pan with a little olive oil and warm the pan.

Take the fish from the oven, present the dish at table, set it on a suitable heatproof surface but don't break the crust yet; if you like, let everyone guess what's hiding underneath.

Quickly get the pan very hot, put in the peppers and stir, so that nothing burns, for 3 minutes or so; when the peppers are hot and crisp, with their colours enhanced by the cooking, bring them to table in the pan and serve them on individual dinner plates; ask your guests to try them while you dish out the fish.

Break the salt crust, removing lumps on top, and, especially, loose salt around the sides – this will take a little while, so be patient or you will end up with rather more salt on the fillets than you might enjoy; with a sharp knife cut along the line of the backbone, fold back the skin and lift out the top fillets, dividing and serving them as you go; lift out the backbone from the back, together with the head, and serve the bottom fillets.

Toss the salad at table; pour a little olive oil first and when the leaves are evenly coated sprinkle over a little lemon juice, salt and black pepper, and finish tossing. Serve with the fontina on the side.

A GREEKISH FEAST

Inspired by some of the food we tasted in
Greece, and guided not least by Rena
Salaman's writing (*Greek Food*, Fontana, 1983),
here is what we would put out on the table
for a party of 4-6 people.

Giant olives

Salted almonds

Stuffed vine leaves

Taramosalata – cod's roe purée

Melitzanosalata – aubergine purée

Tzatziki – cucumber and yoghurt salad

Feta, tomato and black olive salad

Pittas

Peaches, pomegranates and grapes

Retsina

SHOPPING LIST

It's difficult to be precise with a spread of dishes of this kind –
obviously everyone has his or her favourites – but, altogether,

the following quantities should easily feed 4 or even 6. You may want to leave out one or other of the dishes one day, so the necessary ingredients and their quantities are given individually.

OLIVES – Greek Super Mammouth (*sic*) olives, canned by the Kyknos Canning Company, are quite unlike anything else we know – huge, as the name suggests, glistening mauve and satisfyingly fleshy, but beware of the acutely pointed stones; a 1 lb (500 g) can turned into a bowl provides a wonderful extra focus to this spread.

SALTED ALMONDS – buy ready-made in a Greek delicatessen, but make sure they have been kept in airtight containers. Ask to taste one – it ought to be crisp, not damp. Count a handful per head.

STUFFED VINE LEAVES – these, too, you can buy in cans of varying sizes, in supermarkets or specialist shops. Allow at least 4 per person.

TARAMOSALATA – you could buy it ready-made, of course, but here are the principle ingredients for our version, which is quickly made and bears no resemblance in appearance or taste to the commercial product. You will need 8 oz (250 g) smoked cod's roe, preferably not the bright red variety coloured with beetroots; 1 soft white roll or 1 thick slice white bread; a few tablespoons milk; 1 tablespoon finely chopped onion; 2 cloves summer garlic; approximately ¼ pint (150 ml) virgin olive oil; 2 tablespoons lemon juice; black pepper.

MELITZANOSALATA – aubergine purée salad, which you *will* have to make yourself unless you want to forgo its unique taste. You need 2 large aubergines; 1 small onion (or part of the larger one from making the taramosalata); 1 clove of garlic; 1 teaspoon tarragon vinegar or 1 tablespoon lemon juice; 1 tablespoon virgin olive oil; 1 tablespoon real mayonnaise, however use olive oil in preference to bottled mayonnaise; salt and black pepper.

TZATZIKI – cucumber and yoghurt salad. There are many versions of this simple salad, and we have tried not a few of them, but it seems most important to us that you should use real Greek yoghurt, which is in a class of its own. You need half a large cucumber; 1 clove of garlic; 1 tablespoon virgin olive oil; 1 tablespoon lemon juice; a 8 oz (250 g) carton of Greek yoghurt; a few leaves of mint to garnish the salad.

FETA, TOMATO AND OLIVE SALAD – per head count 2 oz (50 g) of feta cheese (see p. 156); 2 medium salad tomatoes or half of the big Mediterranean variety; 6 small black olives; plenty of virgin oil and a little lemon juice for the dressing; black pepper.

PITTAS – buy 2 per head, but look at the date stamp; alternatively serve fresh white bread.

PEACHES, POMEGRANATES AND GRAPES – together make a mouth-watering display, though pomegranates are an acquired taste, with children especially unless you spoon out the fleshy garnet globules for them. Look for big yellow Greek peaches and grapes, as they are increasingly available in this country now Greece has joined the EEC. Include a little lemon juice and sugar for dressing the pomegranate if liked.

WINE – white and occasionally pink retsina from Attika is a taste well worth acquiring, for there are few equally light and refreshing wines for hot days. Kourtaki, made in the traditional way, is our favourite – straw in colour, with a strong nose of pine resin, which is added during fermentation not to preserve but to spice the wine. Be careful, though – once you like the stuff, a bottle will not go far. If you want red as well, or are looking for a resin-less alternative, try a more northern wine from Macedonia – Naoussa, by Boutari, is a wine we like, but retsina *is* better.

PREPARATION AND PRECOOKING

Once again it's difficult to be precise, but a couple of hours should be enough to prepare the dishes listed here. Then they are all put on the table together with bowls of olives, stuffed vine leaves and salted almonds.

Begin with the aubergine purée or melitzanosalata. Preheat your oven to gas 4/350°F/180°C. Meanwhile rinse the aubergines, dry, and prick a few times with a fork so that they won't explode when heated. Place them on a grid shelf in the oven and bake for 45 minutes. Alternatively, put them on a solid shelf and turn them once, half-way through baking.

Make the taramosalata while the aubergines are in the oven. Thinly slice the white roll or chunk of bread, lay the slices in a mixing bowl and sprinkle with enough milk to make the bread soggy, without covering it. Leave for 15 minutes. Meanwhile finely chop 1 tablespoon onion and skin and chop 2 cloves of garlic. Skin the cod's roes, and put them with the onions and garlic in a mortar, pounding until smooth.

Squeeze excess moisture from the bread and amalgamate it, pounding again, bit by bit with the mix in the mortar. Drop by drop add the olive oil, about ¼ pint (150 ml); season with 2 tablespoons lemon juice and black pepper, but no salt – the cod's roe has all the salt you need. Transfer to a suitable bowl and store in the refrigerator until serving. (Note: you could make the taramosalata a day in advance, but on no account use a processor – it would spoil the consistency and texture of the roes.)

Continue with the melitzanosalata. Remove the aubergines from the oven and let them cool, preferably on a grid to prevent condensation.

Start the tzatziki. Peel the cucumber, slice it in half lengthwise and scoop out the seeds with a teaspoon. With a sharp knife cut long strips about ⅛ inch (3 mm) thick, then chop across into dice. Salt slightly and put in a colander to drip.

Finish the melitzanosalata. Peel the aubergines and tear the flesh with a pair of forks. Thinly slice the onion. Peel and crush the clove of garlic. Put all in the mortar, add 1 teaspoon tarragon vinegar or 1 tablespoon lemon juice, and 1 tablespoon olive oil, and pound until roughly smooth. Add 1 tablespoon of home-made mayonnaise if you happen to have some, or a similar quantity of olive oil, plus a little salt and fresh black pepper. Pound a little more and transfer into a bowl from where it is served at room temperature.

Finish the tzatziki. Squeeze the diced cucumber for a minute or so and put it into the bowl you will be offering it in. Peel and crush the clove of garlic, mix it with 1 tablespoon olive oil and 1 teaspoon of lemon juice, pour over the cucumber and mix. Add the Greek yoghurt – an approximately 8 oz (250 g) carton – mix again and put it in the refrigerator until you serve it, garnished with the mint leaves.

Make the tomato and feta salad. Rinse the tomatoes, dry and slice. Arrange the slices on a platter. Dice the feta cheese, approximately 2 oz (50 g) per head, into cubes about ½ inch (1 cm) big and scatter over the tomatoes together with the small black olives. Pour over a little olive oil and a minimum of lemon juice, if any, only at the last moment. Sprinkle with a little black pepper but no salt – the feta, usually stored in brine, is salty enough.

Warm the pittas in the oven, at the same temperature you used to bake the aubergines, for 5 minutes. Wrap them in a napkin or fresh dish cloth before putting them out – they will stay warm for longer that way.

Last, arrange the fruit on a platter or basket, with a bowl of iced water for washing individual helpings on the side. To eat a pomegranate – cut it in half, scoop out lumps of juicy garnet globules with a teaspoon and separate, discarding bitter white pith; add a little sugar and lemon juice if you like.

AUTUMN

GENTLE FLAVOURS, FOR A SUBTLE GRAPE

An uncomplicated, easily prepared meal to accompany a whole range of German rieslings, showing how they vary from region to region, and how age brings out their best.

Quails' eggs and celery salt; salad of red and white chicory, mushrooms and first cob nuts of the season

Sole meunière; purée of potatoes and celeriac

Caerphilly

New pears

German rieslings

SHOPPING LIST

SOLE – an indigenous fish and one of the best, though caught not only off Dover but as far south as the Mediterranean. Tell the fishmonger in advance how many you intend feeding, and to show you the difference between *solea solea* and others that might serve as alternatives, such as sand or French sole, thickback sole and even the lemon sole, though this is related to the flounders and is not a sole at all. The real article is not always available in sufficient quantities, especially if you are planning a bigger party. Sizes vary, of course, with mature specimens reaching 20 inches (50 cm) in length, and here at last is a fish you could just keep in the refrigerator overnight – there are those who insist that a true sole improves for a day or two after it has been caught. Calculate 2 fillets or about 10 oz (300 g) per portion. Unless you intend cooking within a few hours, have the fish gutted but not skinned – it will only dry out – and the head left on.

QUAILS' EGGS – commercially produced, of course, and available from butchers and supermarkets. They usually come in boxes of a dozen, and should be date-stamped; check all are intact; allow 4 per person.

RED CHICORY – or radicchio as it has also become known in our markets over the last few years. Individual heads can be quite small, but they are relatively dense, and the leaves should be tightly wrapped. Buy by eye, counting no more than 2-3 good-size leaves per portion.

WHITE CHICORY – rather more familiar than its red cousin, best in autumn and winter. Look for immaculate white heads, which ought to be heavy and firm, showing almost no green at all. Reject specimens with cut or otherwise damaged leaves. Store in a dark cool place or the leaves will go green. Allow enough leaves to balance the red ones.

BUTTON MUSHROOMS – buy just a few of the smallest you can find, so that they can go raw and whole into the salad, 4-5 per portion. Alternatively choose bigger ones, which will make perfect mushroom shapes when sliced.

NUTS – really new cobnuts come in tight clusters with leaves attached, and are still green outside. You will need less than a handful per helping once shelled, but look for little holes, similar to those made by woodworm – pests, too, like the creamy consistency and subtle flavour of these nuts.

POTATOES – for puréeing, 1 medium to biggish mealy but new potato per head, or 1 lb (500 g) for 4 servings.

CELERIAC – spicy, large turnip-like roots with a delicious celery flavour. 1 big one may easily match 4 potatoes, and approximately similar quantities are what we have in mind, but don't be misled – because of its gnarled and deeply pitted exterior celeriac needs to be skinned thickly and ends up rather smaller in the pot than it may have appeared at first sight.

PEARS – Williams would be best, provided they are ripe, with a strong sweet scent and unblemished bright yellow skins, but Conference, for example, can also be delicious. Treat them carefully once bought – pears bruise easily and deeply, and, once ripe, are prone to go over the top within half a day or so. Refrigerate them if the scent is strong – with this meal they should be quite cold, even icy at first, when served. Ripe nectarines or peaches would be an excellent substitute if on the market.

LEMON – a few drops of lemon juice to dress each portion of the starter.

CAERPHILLY – Welsh originally, but made mainly in Somerset nowadays, though we hear that there are some farms in Wales back in business making small quantities of this subtle cheese. With more than a hint of buttermilk, it is slightly grainy and short in flavour when eaten young – usually too young, the cheese specialists in Neal's Yard in London say. So try for a slightly older and darker cheese – all of twelve weeks or so – and compare it, if you like, with a fresh white specimen.

BUTTER – to cook *à la meunière* ('the miller's wife') means to fry in butter (because millers, who did not always give back in flour all that they had received in grain, tended to be well off?). The butter should be unsalted and fresh, enough to cook with and to melt some more thereafter – about 3 oz (75 g) to fry each sole; plus 1 oz (25 g) per head to make butter sauce, and the same again per portion of the purée.

CREAM – ¼ pint (150 ml) single cream will make purée for 4.

HAZELNUT OIL – allow 2 teaspoons or so for each starter.

FLOUR – allow about 2 oz (50 g) white flour to coat each sole before frying.

CELERY SALT – a brownish mix of fine salt, celery and silika to prevent lumps caused by moisture, available wherever you find dried herbs and spices. A 3 oz (75 g) jar will go far, finding other uses too – in a Bloody Mary, for example.

OTHER INGREDIENTS – a little milk for the purée.

RIESLING – almost everyone *knows* that some hocks and moselles, as they are still called in certain lists, belong among the truly great wines, and, though Germany is expensive, can be excellent value – perhaps because people think they are generally too sweet and will not go with food. But riesling varies from region to region, and improves with age, providing the vintage is good. With this rudimentary knowledge we thought we would ask for advice, and best get it from the horse's mouth – O. W. Loeb & Company Limited, of London and Trier.

Nicholas Clarke was the director at Loeb's patient enough to take the call – we wondered whether he would care to choose the wines for this menu, so that not only would we be able to taste a little of the variety of German rieslings but also of their development with age. Here is what he suggested and we bought, tried *and* liked.

As an aperitif, carrying on into the first course – from the Ruwer, which flows into the Mosel, 1985 Kaseler Nies'chen Riesling Kabinett, Estate-bottled Erben von Beulwitz; 1985 Maximin Grünhauser Abtsberg Kabinett, Estate-bottled C. von Schubert; with the main course – from the Saar, which also feeds the Mosel, 1983 Oberemmeler Scharzberg Riesling Kabinett, Estate-bottled Friedrich Wilhelm Gymnasium; with the cheese – from the Nahe, a tributary of the Rhine, 1979 Münsterer Dautenpflänzer Riesling Spätlese, Estate-bottled Staatliche Weinbaudomäne; with the fruit – from Rheinhessen, 1976 Niersteiner Orbel Riesling Beerenauslese, Estate-bottled Gustav Gessert.

How did we cope with so many bottles? We got four friends to assist, making it less than a bottle per head of these relatively unalcoholic wines. Reduce the aperitif to one wine, and leave out the one suggested for the cheese, if you are planning to entertain a smaller number.

PREPARATION AND PRECOOKING

An hour and a half before the appointed time take the quails' eggs, fish, vegetables and cheese from the refrigerator if there, and make sure your wines are getting cold, though not too cold, especially not the older wines – a cold room might be the right place for them.

With a sharp knife chop the roots from the red chicory, pull off individual leaves and rinse under cold water. Shake dry and put aside in a colander in a cool place.

Chop the root end from the white chicory, break off the outer leaves and discard unless immaculate. Cut off a little more from the root end and inspect the inner leaves to see whether they need washing. Strip the entire head, cutting ends cleanly, and set aside.

Wash the mushrooms and dry with kitchen paper. Trim stems. If the mushrooms are too big to be eaten whole, slice them with a sharp knife – vertically, as thin as you can.

Crack the cobnuts, put them into the salad bowl, pour over a little hazelnut oil, a few drops of lemon juice, and toss to prevent browning.

Wash the potatoes and celeriac and peel with a heavy knife, deeply, as regards the latter. Cut into biggish chunks, put in a saucepan, cover with water and salt and set aside.

Put some water to boil, lid on, for the quails' eggs.

Meanwhile clarify 3 oz (75 g) of butter for each sole you intend frying. Cut cold butter into cubes and melt over low heat in a saucepan. With a flat spoon or spatula skim off white impurities rising to the surface and discard – they would burn at the high temperatures required to fry the fish. Choose a frying pan or pans or similar flat heavy dishes big enough to take a sole each, distribute the clarified butter between them, and set aside.

Put the quails' eggs on a perforated spoon and carefully lower into boiling water. Reduce the heat and simmer for 2 minutes. Remove and plunge into cold water.

Skin the sole or soles. Rinse the fish under cold water first and put it on a flat surface, white side down. With a sharp knife cut across the root of the tail fin – just deep enough to make a slit in the dark upper skin, from side to side. With the point of the knife, work loose a flap, big enough to give you a hold. Press the tail firmly down with the heel of one hand, pulling the skin with the other, towards the head. This may be difficult at first but will become easier as you progress, but make sure the skin comes off across the full breadth, including the fins. Pull the skin over the head, turn the fish and pull the white skin now, in one piece with the dark, back to the tail. Once more rinse the fish under cold water, being careful to get rid of scales which will have worked loose from the dark upper side.

Set the fish aside in a cool place if you are planning to cook only one or two; sole is best cooked on the bone. For a bigger party fillet the skinned clean fish – put it on a board and with a sharp knife cut along the backbone and down to it; put the blade into the incision, flatten it towards the outside and cut away each fillet in turn, keeping as close as possible to the bones; lay the fillets one on top of the other and cover loosely to keep moist.

Arrange the cold dry quails' eggs on individual plates; they look very pretty in their freckled shells, but are fiddly to peel – so 4 may be enough for most people to cope with. Add the whole white and red chicory leaves, mushrooms and nuts to make an attractive display on each plate. Put a little hazelnut oil in a small jug, and some lemon juice in another, ready for serving.

Work out the rest of your timetable – the potatoes and celeriac will need to be brought to the boil, and then cooked for about 15 minutes thereafter, plus 5 minutes or so to purée; the sole or soles will take 3-5 minutes per side to fry.

COOKING AND PRESENTATION

Serve the first course as the potatoes and celeriac are coming to the boil. Don't forget to offer celery salt on the side; eat mainly by hand, dunking salad leaves into oil and only a few drops of lemon juice as you go.

When the potatoes and celeriac chunks are tender, drain them through a colander, and let them and the saucepan dry under their own heat.

Sprinkle the fish, whole or fillets, with milk, salt and fresh black pepper. On a flat surface spread about 2 oz (50 g) of white flour, put the fish down on it, turn over, making a thin coat on both sides, and let it dry for a few moments – preferably on a grill rack, a double layer of kitchen paper otherwise – the flour will stick to the fish better if dry.

Return the potato and celeriac chunks to the saucepan you cooked them in, over low heat. Add a good knob of butter, let it melt, and mash roughly. Add a little of the cream, and continue mashing and mixing until all the butter and cream are worked in and the purée is quite smooth. Take from the heat and let it sit, lid on, for a minute or two if necessary.

Meanwhile heat the clarified butter for frying the fish, over high heat. Put in the sole or soles as the butter is about to smoke – it should sizzle, the fish absorbing excess heat instantly. Watch, adjusting the heat if necessary – the underside should reach an even golden brown without the butter smoking much again after 4 minutes if the fish is whole, less than 2 if filleted; turn and cook for not quite the same time again. Always turn whole fish with two flat tools – fish slices or spatulas – at the same time, being careful not to break it.

When the fish is done, put single portion fishes on individual plates, bigger ones on plates they can be filleted on, and pour away the butter you were cooking in. Don't wash or scrape the pan but return it to a hot heat. Quickly melt the butter for the sauce – about 1 oz (25 g) per portion – until it turns brown. Pour it over the fish and serve with the purée in a separate serving bowl.

Fillet bigger whole fish at table. Hold the fish with the back of a fork. With a pointed knife cut down and along the backbone and around the fins on either side of the body. Insert the blade along the backbone again and slide it, as flat as possible now, over the bones towards the sides. Lift out the top fillets; pick up the back bone by the tail and discard, together with the head; serve the bottom fillets, offering the fins to those inclined to pick away at the tasty little pieces of flesh attached to their bones.

Serve the caerphilly, with its own wine if your party is big enough.

Last, take the pears from the refrigerator, rinse under cold water, and dry. With a razor sharp knife slice them vertically, as thin as you can. Lay out these whole slices on individual plates, sprinkle with a little fresh black pepper and serve with knives and forks, with the pudding wine on the side. Alternatively, peel and dice chilled nectarines or peaches; put each fruit in a separate glass, pour over a little of the pudding wine, serve with spoons and eat immediately.

FOR AN INDIAN SUMMER DAY

A meal suitable for outdoor cooking if you like, and easily adapted for a larger party. Few people seem to know about grilling corn on the cob whole, but Gerd grew up in the country in Austria surrounded by fields of these handy little food parcels – a little fire and salt were all he and his friends needed to enjoy them at their best.

Corn on the cob

Grilled lamb chops

Salad of new leeks, with mustard dressing

Brown bread ice cream

Vin de pays

SHOPPING LIST

LAMB CHOPS – ask for indigenous chump chops, from the back end of a young animal that has never been frozen. The meat should be pink rather than dark, with hardly any fat. Buy 1 chop, no more than 1 inch (2.5 cm) thick, per person.

CORN ON THE COB – look for smallish ears that have been cut only a day or two ago. Check that the green husks are intact, not only because they will have prevented loss of moisture, but also because they will help protect the ears when grilling. Buy 1 per head.

LEEKS – get little thin ones, so that 3 make no more than 1 helping, with fine white ends and crisp green tops.

GARLIC – 1-2 cloves to rub over the chops.

BROWN BREAD ICE CREAM – for 4 helpings you will need ½ pint (300 ml) double cream; 1 oz (25 g) vanilla sugar (alternatively use 3-4 drops of vanilla essence and 1 oz (25 g) white sugar); 3 oz (75 g) stale but not mouldy brown bread from a loaf or roll; a little butter to grease a baking tray; 3 oz (75 g) soft dark brown sugar; a few tablespoons whisky or brandy to pour sparingly over the ice cream. (Make vanilla sugar simply by keeping a vanilla pod in your sugar jar. After a few days the sugar takes on a wonderful scent, welcome with most things in need of sweetening, while the pod will last for months.)

BUTTER – for the corn on the cob, 1 oz (25 g) or so each.

MUSTARD – a few teaspoons of powder for the salad dressing.

OLIVE OIL – extra virgin would be best, but a lesser grade will do; a few tablespoons depending on the size of the salad, plus a little more to rub the chops and to cook the leeks.

TARRAGON VINEGAR – a few teaspoons.

WINE – with some 150 official French vins de pays, and not a few of them pressing for higher VDQS (vin de qualité supérieure) and even AC (appellation controlée) status, what to choose, how much to pay? Here, giving an idea just how wide the field is, are the all red three-star choices, taking into account both quality and value for money, tasted in April 1986 by WINE magazine: Vin de Pays des Collines de la Moure, Domaine de l'Abbaye de Valmagne, Cuvée Cardinale 1981; Vin de Pays de l'Hérault, Mas de Daumas Gassac 1983; Vin de Pays de l'Herault, Merlot 1983, Dulong Frères et Fils; Vin de Pays d'Oc, Etablissements Skalli; Vin de Pays des Pyrenées Orientales, Merlot Les 4 Saisons; Vin de Pays des Sables du Golfe de Lion, Listel Rubis.

PREPARATION AND PRECOOKING

Make the brown bread ice cream a day or more in advance, though a few hours in a fast freezer will do.

First whip the cream and vanilla sugar together with an electric or wire whisk until stiff. Be careful not to overbeat, though, especially if using an electric whisk – stop just as soon as you see the first pointed peaks forming. Put in the freezer, in a suitable plastic container.

Preheat the oven to gas 6/400°F/200°C. Meanwhile break up the stale brown bread or roll, put the pieces in a processor and cut into crumbs. Lightly butter a baking tray, spread out the crumbs, and top with the brown sugar. Put the tray in the hot oven, stirring at 5 minute intervals until the sugar caramelizes with the bread – you will notice the smell of caramel – after 15-20 minutes or so. Remove the tray from the oven and set aside to cool.

Take the whipped cream from the freezer, stir in the cold crumbs and return to the freezer. Stir again after 1 hour, breaking up ice crystals along sides and in corners; repeat after another hour, and leave for a minimum of 3 hours in all in the freezer.

An hour before the appointed time, take the lamb chops, corn on the cob and leeks from the refrigerator. If you are planning to grill outdoors, start the fire. Put the chops on a flat surface, crush a clove or two of garlic, and rub the chops with a little olive oil and the garlic. Turn them over after a while, rubbing them with the oil-garlic mix once or twice more.

Precook the leeks. With a sharp knife, trim the white and green ends, slitting the latter 1-2 inches (2.5-5 cm) to see whether any earth has been trapped between the leaves. Rinse and dry if necessary. Cover the bottom of a heavy frying pan with olive oil and place over high heat. When the oil is hot, put in the leeks and stir – they may brown here and there, but they should not burn, and the oil must never smoke. Continue stir-frying for several minutes, depending on thickness – the leeks should taste cooked but still be crunchy by the time you take them off the heat. Let them cool in their oil while you prepare their dressing.

Make a generous amount of mustard dressing, enough to marinade the leeks thoroughly. Put mustard powder, a pinch or two of salt and a little black pepper in a mixing bowl, breaking up dry lumps if any. Add a few drops of the tarragon vinegar and stir until absorbed. Gradually add the rest of the vinegar, and keep stirring until you have a smooth paste. Let it rest for 10 minutes.

Prepare the corn on the cob for grilling. Carefully open up the green husks without breaking them or, worse still, pulling them off. Remove the silk underneath, until all strings have gone. Put the husks back in place, so that the corn on the cob itself is quite covered, around as well as up and down each length. Moisten the husks with a little water if they are at all dry, and put aside under a damp cloth.

Finish making the mustard dressing. Once more stir the mustard and vinegar paste, making sure it's smooth, and whisk in some olive oil – about three parts oil to one of mustard paste – until you have a thickish emulsion of only limited stability. Lay the leeks, which may still be warm, into a suitable serving bowl, pour over the oil you fried them in, and pour the mustard dressing on top. Toss carefully until all the surfaces are well coated. Repeat three or four times, rolling each leek in the dressing.

Last check the fire – it needs to be quite hot for grilling corn on the cob – or think of preheating an electric or gas grill in time.

COOKING AND PRESENTATION

Put the corn on the cob on the sizzling hot grill and watch throughout, turning the cobs as the husks brown. Increase the distance from the source of heat if they threaten to char or catch fire. Cooking times obviously depend also on freshness and moisture contained in the corn itself, but 10 minutes should be enough in most cases. Serve immediately, and eat by hand with salt and cold butter on the side – put a sliver of butter on the cob before each bite or so.

Once more spread the oil and garlic over the chops by rubbing them with your hands; salt slightly and pepper on both sides. Put them on the grill for 1 minute, still at maximum heat; turn without piercing and continue at maximum heat for 1 more minute, when both sides will be sealed, preventing loss of moisture; immediately reduce heat to about three quarters (alternatively, increase their distance from the source of heat) and continue to grill without turning the chops again – they should be done, still a little pink inside, after a further 4 (making a total of 6) minutes. Offer them on a platter or direct on individual plates, serving the leek salad on the side.

Take the brown bread ice cream from the freezer as you sit down to eat the main course.

Serve the ice cream with a little whisky or brandy on each helping.

BARBECUE

A menu you can easily add to for a bigger party, with some of the grills described elsewhere in this book – poussins, pork chops, whole corn on the cob, for example – but which can be cooked indoors if circumstances demand.

Baked potatoes, with sour cream and chives dressing

Spare ribs; spicy sausages

Guacamole

Cheeses from Savoy and Dauphiné

Salad of new apples, pears, grapes, bananas and nuts of the season

Australian wines

SHOPPING LIST

POTATOES – 1 new baking potato per head, with its skin intact.

CHIVES – approximately 1 tablespoon of chopped chives per potato.

FRUIT FOR THE SALAD – apples, pears, grapes, bananas, nuts – inspect what's on offer, especially among domestic fruit. Tart little Cox's and sweet but firm Conference pears, with creamy new walnuts or cobnuts, a banana plus some imported muscat grapes, yellow and black – buy entirely by eye and nose, as good fresh fruit always has a tempting scent. Substitute or add as you please, but try to balance textures, colours, sweet and acid – many a fruit salad fails in super-abundance. Try to judge quantities by imagining a single portion – a little apple and half a pear, a few banana slices plus a handful each of grapes and nuts. As with all dishes of the kind, the ingredients are cut up, of course; nonetheless insist on perfect fruit with bright unblemished skins. For the dressing buy a lime or small lemon, plus half a small orange per portion.

GUACAMOLE – a number of tasty concoctions travel under this name, derived from Nahuatl *ahuacamolli* via American Spanish, meaning avocado and sauce. Here are the ingredients for one version we like, but see also the simpler purer recipe Liz picked up in Mexico itself (see p. 181). For 2 portions you will need 1 salad tomato; 1 tablespoon each of chopped sweet green pepper, celery and onion; 1 clove of garlic; 1 ripe avocado; 1 tablespoon of lime or lemon juice, plus extra for sprinkling the avocados; a few coriander or basil leaves; 2 tablespoons of virgin olive oil.

SOUR CREAM – ¼ pint (150 ml) will dress 2 big potatoes.

CHEESE – beaufort, reblochon, Saint-Marcellin are three names from Savoy and Dauphiné you might ask for. Beaufort, of the gruyère family of cheeses but richer and with fissures instead of holes, is praised above its relations by some. Reblochon, once upon a time fraudulently made from the second milking of cows, or so the story goes, is softer and creamier than the first, and available in two rather smaller sizes. Finally Saint-Marcellin from the Dauphiné, little cheeses allegedly made famous by none less than Louis XI, with a vivid orange and grey mould, which used to be made exclusively from goat's milk but today can be pure cow's.

SPARERIBS – a popular cut not only in Chinese restaurants, from inside the thick front end of the belly, and not to be confused with the synonymous but rather meatier cut from the neck of the animal. Count 3 ribs per head. Order in advance if your party is going to be a big one, and bring your purchase home 24 hours before, so that you can salt it overnight in order to improve its flavour.

SAUSAGES – many butchers have their own recipes for spicy pork sausages, especially in the country, so ask around a little if necessary and buy by eye, about 1 or 2 per person depending on size, but do make sure it isn't last week's production you are carrying home in a hot car – pork sausages are made with uncooked meat, and though usually highly salted and spiced, need to be quite fresh.

SALT – sea salt, fresh ground black pepper and dried herbs are what you need to cure the spareribs. You will need salt, above all, in sufficient quantity – about 1 lb (500 g) for each cut of 6 spare ribs.

WINE – Australia is the place often associated with barbecues, so why not try one or two of her simpler, sturdier wines with this meal? For example, from Adnam's list, in Southwold, Suffolk, try a fresh Muscat Blanc, which is quite dry, by Brown Bros at Milawa, Victoria; followed by red 1981 Kalimna, Bin 28, Shiraz by Penfolds, South Australia; and finish with a late picked 1982 Muscat of Alexandra, by Baileys at Glenrowan, Victoria.

PREPARATION AND PRECOOKING

Salt the spareribs so that they can improve in flavour overnight. First find an earthenware or glass dish to hold the meat, in two or more layers if necessary. Mix the sea salt, fresh black pepper and some dried herbs in a bowl. Cover the bottom of the salting dish with this mix, put the spareribs on top, sprinkle with plenty of the salt mix and rub gently, leaving a good layer of the salt on top. Proceed with additional cuts in similar fashion, and put them all in a cool place. Turn the spareribs over after a few hours or so, changing their position, and again until you find some brine in the dish, drawn from the meat. Pour off the brine and continue as before.

An hour before your party – a little earlier if big – scrub the potatoes in cold water until they are quite clean; remove eyes and other blemishes from the skins but leave them intact as far as possible for eating. Let them dry, sprinkle with salt and put in the oven at gas 6/400°F/200°C – there is no need to preheat, a medium-large potato will take approximately 1 hour.

At the same time, take the cheeses from the refrigerator and make sure the white wines go in. Get the fire going if you are barbecueing outdoors.

Now make the guacamole, quantities as given in the shopping list or in proportion. First peel the tomatoes – bring some water to the boil in a kettle and pour over the tomatoes in a bowl to scald but not cook them. With a sharp knife, nick the skins and pull off – they should come away quite readily.

When the tomatoes are peeled, cut them in half, scoop out the seeds with a spoon and discard, chop coarsely and then set aside.

Wash the green pepper, cut it in half, discarding white membranes and seeds, and chop finely.

Wash the celery, pull off strings and chop finely.

Peel the onion and the garlic, crushing the latter under a knife blade first. Chop finely together.

Cut the avocado in half, discard stones and scoop out the flesh with a spoon. Immediately sprinkle with lime or lemon juice to prevent browning and mash with a fork – don't use a blender for guacamole, as it will taste bland if too smooth.

Combine all the various ingredients in a mixing bowl, including the chopped coriander, and adding a little more lime or lemon juice, enough olive oil to make a thick paste, pepper and salt. Mix thoroughly with a fork, cover and put into the refrigerator until serving.

Make the fruit salad last. Squeeze the lime or lemon and oranges, strain, and mix to make the dressing. Wash the fruit under cold water and let drip dry in a colander. Sharpen a stainless steel knife (blunt knives bruise and squash; carbon steel blades discolour fruit and vegetables, leaving an unpleasant metallic taste on their cut surfaces).

Peel the apples, quarter vertically, cut out cores, and quickly chop further still, slicing them into firm little dice. Place them in a bowl suitable for serving – glass, china or earthenware – sprinkle with a little of the dressing to prevent browning, and turn over once or twice. Be careful not to blunt the fruits' points and edges – throughout composition, work gently. The less you toss it, the more appetizing your salad will look, with glistening shiny pieces of fruit and clear rather than cloudy juices. (Contrary to what is sometimes written, fresh fruit does not improve by being steeped in liquids for long times, nor are strong alcohols good companions for them. Fresh, as opposed to dried fruit salads, should be crisp when served, finally mixing only in the eater's mouth as it were; fruit bowls and drinks like sangria, too, are best made quite fresh, a few minutes before serving.)

Do the pears next, in similar fashion, then the bananas and grapes, slicing them in halves. Discard grape pips if they bother you, and shell the nuts. Sprinkle the halved walnuts and whole cobnuts over the salad, together with the rest of your dressing. Cover and put into the refrigerator.

Finely chop the chives, mix with the sour cream and leave in a cool place.

Last, wipe the spareribs with a clean cloth, removing any salt that may still be sticking to them. Rub them with a little olive oil and set aside, ready for grilling. Take the sausages from the refrigerator, unwrap and prick here and there – two or three times will do – with a tooth pick or thin-pronged fork, so that they won't burst when heated.

COOKING AND PRESENTATION

Start grilling the spareribs on medium to highish heat, or at a good distance if your fire is very hot. Brown one side, then the other, and turn again several times, basting with a little extra oil as necessary; depending on their thickness they should be done after 25 minutes or so.

Meanwhile serve the baked potatoes, as a starter, with the cream and chives dressing on the side.

Begin grilling the sausages in similar fashion – but without basting as they contain their own fat – when the spareribs are half done. Offer the sausages as soon as they are ready.

Cut the spareribs on a board with a heavy knife, serving 3 per head. Offer the guacamole on the side, instead of a spicy barbecue sauce.

Serve the cheeses and, finally, the fruit salad with a glass of sweet wine – those fabled Australian liqueur muscats go well with gentle fruit.

FIRST MUSSELS

September brings back mussels on the market, and there are few tastier recipes for them than this simple soup. It's easily made and plentiful enough, especially if you have more than one stilton to offer at the end. Serve some smoked fish, such as eel and sturgeon, before or after the soup if you are worried about appetites not being satisfied. You will need a piece of muslin cloth for straining the soup.

Mussel soup with saffron

Salad of new oranges, sweet onions and olives

Blue and white stilton

Joao Pires 1985 White Palmela, Muscat

Croft 1978 late bottled vintage port, or 1980 Masi Classico Amarone Recioto della Valpolicella

SHOPPING LIST

MUSSELS – for the soup. Buy them alive, 3 lb (1.5 kg) for 4 helpings; get them home quickly, letting them sit wrapped in damp newspaper, in a cool place if necessary.

OTHER INGREDIENTS FOR THE SOUP – for 4 servings you will need 2 tablespoons of finely chopped onion; 1 oz (25 g) butter; a few sprigs of thyme, fresh if available, otherwise make do with dried; ¾ pint (450 ml) good dry white wine; salt and pepper; 1 tiny packet of saffron threads, containing 125 milligrams or so; 4 egg yolks; 1 pint (600 ml) double cream.

RYE BREAD – traditionally served with smoked salmon, this would go well with the soup, but good fresh white may be just as tasty.

ORANGES – look for sweetish ones, from the new southern European harvest. Make sure they are firm with bright skins – as with other fruit, old remnants will stray into new deliveries. Count 1 orange per portion.

ONIONS – big sweet Spanish onions, which make attractive blue and white rings, are best. Count 1 thickish slice per portion to give you an idea how much you might need for the salad.

OLIVES – allow a good mixed handful of black and green per portion of the salad.

OLIVE OIL – a few tablespoons of extra virgin for the salad, depending on the number of helpings.

CHEESES – "Good blue stilton ready to eat has the protection of an uncracked, tough, hard crust; the interior is cream-coloured to yellow, not white, and its veins reveal a well spread greeny blue rather than blue-black or cindery aspect. The texture varies largely with the tightness of packing of the curd in the hoop, and offers a range from crumbly to smooth, from soft to firm, wide enough to suit many different palates. I am thankful for this as I iron my Christmas cheeses, and match their potential characters with the specified requirements of my splendidly demanding customers." So says Patrick Rance (*The Great British Cheese Book*, Papermac, 1983) with the experience of one who has not only researched and eaten but also sold this English classic for many years. So approach your cheese merchant, perhaps not demanding but with your eyes open, asking for advice and a taste of this or that cheese. Buy from more than one cheese if you can, with a little white stilton for contrast if you like.

WINE – what to drink with a mussel soup containing wine already, and then with stilton? We thought of sherry, a salty manzanilla matured in the sea breeze ventilated bodegas of Sanlucar, and wondered whether there might be an old oloroso that could take the role of port traditionally served with stilton, but even the people at Gonzalez Byass thought there wasn't. Madeira was the next route to be explored. What about rainwater, followed by bual?, asked Gerd on the telephone to one illustrious house. Sercial and malmsey much better was the reply. More consultations – Alastair Marshall, of Adnams in Southwold, didn't believe in big wines with big food if they were likely to interfere with each other; a dry recioto amarone might be a good idea, but, anyway, he wouldn't be eating stilton in the first place . . . Sue Cloke, General Manager of Paxton & Whitfield, who sell perhaps more stilton than anyone else in London: "An Englishman who doesn't like stilton? An early bottled vintage port, or a claret, that's what you ought to try, comparing various stiltons, pasteurized versus unpasteurized . . ." Only half a revolution – i.e. away from vintage port proper – suggested here then, whatever may be going on in the battlefields of new wines and food. We liked the port, though Masi's 1980 recioto amarone is not a bad idea at all, indeed it's a great wine, bettered only by his amarone mazzano. As for that white muscat fom Portugal, we heard it's made by a young Australian, and is a most perfumed, drinkable light delight.

PREPARATION AND PRECOOKING

You could make the basis for the soup in advance, refrigerating the cooked mussels for the better part of the day (but not overnight) in between. The quantity and state of mussels to be cleaned is obviously a major factor as regards time – we reckon it takes 20-30 minutes to clean 3 lb (1.5 kg) mussels if they are reasonably clean to start with.

Clean the mussels under running cold water. Discard those with broken shells as well as whole ones which will not close even when tapped. With a sharp short knife scrape off barnacles and pull away beards. Put the mussels in a colander and set aside in a cool place.

Finely chop the 2 tablespoons of onion. In a large saucepan heat the butter and cook the onion with a few sprigs of thyme until soft. Add two thirds of the white wine and heat until steaming. Turn the heat to maximum, add the mussels, reduce the heat slightly and leave them to steam for 5 minutes, lid on, shaking vigorously every minute.

Strain over a bowl to reserve the mussel liquor. Check all the shells have opened, discarding those that have not, and let cool. Strain the mussel liquor through a sieve lined with a piece of muslin and reserve. Remove the mussels from their shells and set aside.

Reheat the mussel liquor. Correct with salt and fresh black pepper. Dissolve the saffron in a little hot water and add it to the liquid in the saucepan, together with the remaining third of wine. You can stop here if necessary, refrigerating the mussels and soup base separately.

Then, a few minutes before the first guests are to arrive, peel and slice the onion for the orange salad, so that you get rings about ⅛ inch (3 mm) thick if the onion is really sweet, rather thinner if sharp. Peel and slice the oranges with a sharp knife, a little thicker than the onion, making sure you remove the white pith. Lay the orange slices on a big flat plate or platter, cover with the onion rings, and set aside in a cool place.

Last, take the cheeses from the refrigerator.

COOKING AND PRESENTATION

Finish the soup just before serving it. Take the mussels from the refrigerator, if there. Heat the base of the soup until it begins to boil; meanwhile, in a mixing bowl, whisk the egg yolks and cream.

Turn off the heat. Take a ladle of the soup base and gradually whisk it into the combined yolks and cream in the mixing bowl. Now reverse the process, stirring the mix in the mixing bowl into the egg, cream and broth, and begin to heat through gently. Do not let the soup boil. Add the mussels for the final 2 minutes or so and serve without delay.

Pour a little virgin oil over the orange and onion salad, sprinkle with fresh black pepper but no salt, add the olives and serve.

Offer the stiltons last, with a glass of port or recioto at room temperature.

A TUSCAN SUNDAY LUNCH

An expansive meal, as you might be served in one of the family-run trattorie tucked away in the Chianti hills. Give it time, not so much for preparing or cooking but for enjoying it at a leisurely pace.

Tagliatelle with funghi porcini

Florentine-style steak; salad of red and white chicory

Parmesan

White and black muscat grapes; wet walnuts

1982 Riserva Poliziano, Vino Nobile di Montepulciano
1980 Avignonesi, Vin Santo

SHOPPING LIST

TAGLIATELLE – flat pasta ribbons. Try to buy fresh pasta, half white and half green if you like mixing the colours. Allow about 3 oz (75 g) per person. If you have to make do with the dried kind choose eggy yellow rather than white noodles, allowing a little less in weight per person.

FUNGHI PORCINI – ceps, or wild mushrooms – *boletus edulis* to give them their scientific name. 1 oz (25 g) dried wild mushrooms, available in sachets or loose, is enough for 4 helpings.

BEEFSTEAK – to be grilled Florentine-style. Order the meat in advance. If necessary explain what it is you want – similar to a T-bone but from a *vitellone*, a large calf or an animal two years old. Ask for the steaks to be cut 1 inch (2.5 cm) thick, so that one makes no more than a single portion, but don't worry if that proves impossible – it's quite normal in Tuscany for a steak to be shared by two people.

RED AND WHITE CHICORY – allow 1 small head per person, half red, half white. The red chicory should be tightly closed, showing no signs of going brown at the edges. Only the very tips of the white chicory may be slightly green. Red chicory, now also grown in Britain, is often called by the Italian name radicchio, but in Tuscany you can also find green radicchio. As alternatives use any fresh leaf salad, oak leaf and four seasons to name two.

LEMONS – for the quarter wedges traditionally served with Tuscan grills, as well as for the salad dressing. Choose firm but ripe fruit, with a pleasantly luminous rind.

FRUIT – green muscat grapes and contrasting black ones, and walnuts which are still wet. As an alternative to grapes you might try pomegranates or persimmons – the choice is often one of supply rather than seasons. Buy by eye – ripe green grapes display a waxy yellow tinge; brown marks show they may have been damaged by frost if they are not rotting. Avoid perfect-to-look-at but tasteless black hot-house grapes. Make sure the walnuts are a moist creamy white when broken – if not it's better not to buy.

DOUBLE CREAM – ½ pint (300 ml) for 4 servings of tagliatelle.

PARMESAN – parmigiano-reggiano, hand-made in the provinces of Parma, Reggio, Mantua, Modena and Bologna. Look out for the real article, easily recognizable by the name written all over the rind, though ordinary *grana* can also be delicious. Ask whether the piece you buy is of first quality and has only just been cut – it should be slightly yellow rather than a dry white.

WINES – for many years, when in Tuscany, we have been buying wines from the Azienda Agricola Poliziano in the Piazza Grande right at the very top of breath-taking Montepulciano – red, of course, but also white, pink and vin santo – and we are beginning to find them in London as well. To us they have always been outstanding wines, a clear cut above most chiantis with which they must share much of the prescribed make-up, proving nonetheless that vino nobile can be a denomination in its own right. Now we hear that Maurizio Castelli has taken over wine-making there, and things may improve further still.

The vin santo from neighbours and rivals Avignonesi is a wine Nicholas Belfrage (*Life Beyond Lambrusco*, Sidgwick & Jackson, 1985) has compared with grande champagne cognac in colour and bouquet, rating it as one of Italy's greats – yes, we like it, but be prepared to pay even more than for cognac. On a less exalted level Poliziano, too, make vin santo well worth consideration, but at a quarter of the price.

PREPARATION AND PRECOOKING

An hour or so before the first guest is likely to arrive, put the dried mushrooms in a small bowl and just cover them with water. Stir once or twice, and leave in a warm place.

Start the fire unless you are going to use an electric or gas grill. Use small pieces of wood – holm oak is what many of the traditional recipes say – rather than commercial charcoal if you can.

Take the meat from the refrigerator, cover and let it warm to room temperature. Remove the cheese from the refrigerator if you have not been able to store it in a cool place, arrange them on a platter or plate, cover loosely and leave to warm just slightly.

Arrange the unwashed fruit and nuts in a basket or on a serving plate.

Clean the salad leaves – cut remains of roots from the red chicory, bitter cores from the white. Remove the outer leaves which may be sandy, wash and dab dry with a paper towel. Unwrap the inner leaves which should be clean enough as they are. Put into a generous bowl and leave in a cool place.

Lift out the soaked funghi porcini, squeezing them over their bowl. Save the liquor and finely chop the mushrooms. In a small pan heat a little butter. Gently fry the funghi, until they have absorbed the butter. Add the strained mushroom liquor to the pan, stirring at low heat until nearly dry. Add the cream, stir, correct the seasoning with a little salt and fresh black pepper and set aside.

Last, fill a big saucepan with plenty of water – a gallon (4.5 litres) for 4 helpings of tagliatelle or so. Add salt, cover and set to boil in good time.

COOKING AND PRESENTATION

Check the embers of the fire are deep and wide-spread enough, or turn an electric or gas grill to maximum. Warm up a generous bowl for mixing and serving the tagliatelle. Get everyone moving to the table.

Cook the pasta. If fresh, drop the tagliatelle into fast boiling water, stir, let the water return to the boil and immediately reduce to a simmer. Watch the tagliatelle return to the surface – test after 3 minutes, when they should be nearly done. If cooking dry pasta, don't reduce the water to a simmer but let it boil at high heat, stirring to keep apart strands that may have stuck together; test after about 8 or 9 minutes; pasta is cooked when there is still a little resistance left to the bite – *al dente*.

Drain the cooked pasta through a colander and put into the warm bowl with a little butter. Without reheating first, add the porcini and cream. Toss and serve without delay.

Grilling the meat – most traditional recipes insist that a bistecca fiorentina should not be seasoned in advance. Assuming the steaks are approximately 1 inch (2.5 cm) thick, set the grill about three times that distance above the embers (or under the source of heat if using an indoor grill), which by now should be very hot indeed. Put the meat on the grill to seal for 1 minute. Turn, seal and continue to cook on the same side for 4 minutes. Turn for the last time and cook just for 1 more minute, 6 in all for a rare steak, 8 for medium – but no longer or the meat will be dry. (If the steaks are rather thicker, increase both the distance of the grill from the fire and the cooking time, or the meat will burn on the surface without being done inside.) Season with salt and black pepper. Carve the steaks if they are really big, separating loin and tenderloin, which have different textures; serve a mixture of both, with a wedge of lemon on each plate.

Pause a little before the salad. Bring in the bowl from the cool. Tear but don't cut the bigger leaves. Add plenty of oil – a generous man; pour a little wine vinegar or lemon – a miser; toss vigorously, preferably with your hands, alternatively with blunt wooden tools – like a madman. Those are the three men Italians say it takes to make a good salad.

Serve the cheeses, fruit, nuts and Vin Santo.

MAINLY RED AND GREEN

A light menu, with a minimum of preparation
and cooking time.

Hot artichokes with butter

Grilled red mullet; braised celeriac

Tarte aux pommes from the pâtisserie counter

Selection of Chablis

SHOPPING LIST

RED MULLET – a Mediterranean fish, found in south English waters all the same and so also available fresh to us. There are two kinds, *mullus barbatus* and *mullus surmuletus*, which differ in size more than anything else – the first is smaller, up to 10 inches (25 cm) long, which would be a perfect single portion fish; *surmuletus* grows up to 16 inches (40 cm) long, and is distinguished by a slighty more rounded head and stripes on the two rather spiky tail fins. Both of them have firm white flesh, and are cooked traditionally with their livers – a taste we don't share. Look for brightly coloured fish – pink or red – with shiny red eyes that have lost none of their roundness and stare straight back at you. If you can, choose single portion fish, of either variety, size as described. By all means try the liver, but have the fish scaled and gutted otherwise.

ARTICHOKES – of the thistle family, available again in autumn after a short absence in late summer. Look for round globes, well closed with strong stems – 1 per starter.

CELERIAC – the root of a celery relation, earthy and unsightly, but with a spicy flavour all of its own. It should weigh heavy in the hand and be firm to the touch; don't forget that not a little of that weight will be lost in peeling. Look at a root and imagine how much you will need to make the single vegetable to go with the fish – probably about a quarter of a root per portion. Don't worry if you end up with a little too much – dressed celeriac keeps well in the refrigerator, and makes an excellent starter.

LEMONS – 1 to acidulate the artichoke water; plus some more for the celeriac and to make finger bowls – a quarter of a lemon each.

TARTE AUX POMMES – if you have a local baker, might you order what you need now that the new harvest of apples is coming on the market? Alternatively look around pâtisserie counters and buy what looks fresh, or ask if you are not sure – fruit flans should be eaten on the day they have been made to be at their best.

BUTTER – fresh unsalted or slighty salted butter to go with the artichokes – about 1 oz (25 g) per portion, plus a little to go on the pasta and to fry the celeriac.

DIJON MUSTARD – 1 tablespoon or so for the celeriac.

OLIVE OIL – a little extra virgin, if possible, for the fish.

WINES – there used to be a time when more or less any dry white wine from France and elsewhere was liable to be passed off as Chablis in British restaurants, especially if it was thin and without colour. The real thing is different, with a character to be taken lightly only if you settle for the base product – basic Chablis green and simple, which you might serve as an aperitif and with the first course. Step up one or two levels of quality with the fish, and things become more serious, pleasantly so. There are many names, and here are the top seven, which constitute the whole of the grand crus – Bougros, Les Preuses, Vaudesir, Grenouilles, Valmur, Les Clos and Blanchots. Ask for advice from a merchant who goes to Chablis, especially as regards the two dozen or so premier crus below them, or look for the name of a reputable shipper on the label, such as Joseph Drouhin. In any case go for older wines – like its more southern cousins, the big whites of Burgundy, Chablis is made exclusively from chardonnay grapes, which need time, traditionally in oak and bottle, to show their best.

PREPARATION AND PRECOOKING

Unwrap the fish as soon as you get home and put it on a flat surface. With a razor-sharp knife, make two or three parallel incisions – not too deep – diagonally across the meatiest part of the bodies and tails, on both sides. Pour on a little olive oil and rub it gently over the whole fish and into the cuts which will help to get heat more quickly to the core. Put the oiled fish on a flat plate, cover loosely with greaseproof paper or foil, and put in the refrigerator or a cool place unless you are going to grill it very soon.

An hour before the party, rather less if it is small, wash the artichokes in plenty of cold water, making sure nothing is trapped between the leaves especially if there are gaps. Trim the stems back to the base but don't throw them away – the top end is perfectly edible if stringed, which you can do after cooking.

Wash the celeriac and peel with a sturdy knife, round and round, deeper where pits demand. Quarter the root with a bigger knife and chop into matchstick strips. Sprinkle with a little lemon juice, toss, and set aside in a cool place.

In a big enamelled or stainless steel pan, set enough water to boil for the artichokes, well salted, lid on, allowing up to 20 minutes for 1 gallon (4.5 litres) or so. Put about 1 oz (25 g) butter for each artichoke into a small saucepan, ready to melt.

Cook the celeriac. Melt a good knob of butter in a frying pan, and cook the sticks on medium heat for about 7 minutes, stirring frequently. Take off the heat, cover, and set aside in the pan.

Last, lay on the table one or more big plates to take the debris of artichoke leaves, lay knives and forks for the chokes, and prepare finger baths – a small bowl of warmish water, a chunk of lemon, and an extra napkin each.

COOKING AND PRESENTATION

Begin to cook the artichokes as you serve aperitifs. Squeeze the juice of a lemon into the boiling water, drop in the artichokes, let come back to the boil for a minute or two, then simmer, lid on, for 20 minutes or so, depending on size. Add the stalks about 10 minutes from the end. Test by pulling off an outer leaf – the thick end should be soft when done, not soggy. Drain through a colander and let drip, upside down, while you melt the butter. Serve the artichokes on individual plates, and offer fresh black pepper and melted butter in a sauce boat or small jug. Eat by hand, pulling away the leaves, and discarding hard upper bits.

Preheat the grill for the fish to maximum heat.

Meanwhile finish the celeriac. Reheat the pan, with the sticks still in it. For a quantity of celeriac to serve 4, add 1 tablespoon Dijon mustard, the same of white wine vinegar, a little salt and fresh black pepper; stir vigorously, and cook for a further 2-3 minutes until soft but still firm to the bite. Turn into a serving dish and set aside.

Baste the mullet once more with a little olive oil, and place under or over the hot grill – the thinner the fish, the closer to the heat. Watch carefully – the fish should cook quickly, about 3-4 minutes a side, but not burn. Turn carefully, preferably with two flat tools. Serve from the grill on individual plates, with the celeriac in its own dish.

Offer a little more Chablis, then the tarte aux pommes.

COMFORT

Nursery food almost, Mediterranean-style.

Small salad of feta, chicory and black olives

Prawn pilaf, with Greek yoghurt

Petits pots de chocolat

Gran Viña Sol, Penedes, Miguel Torres

SHOPPING LIST

PRAWNS – buy them cooked in their shells, at least 10 per portion, from a fishmonger with a fast turnover. Reject prawns with a penetrating high smell; take your purchase home quickly and keep in the refrigerator.

VEGETABLES FOR THE PILAF – courgettes, red, yellow or green sweet peppers, small leeks, garlic and tomatoes will give both colour and extra flavour to the rice, in smallish quantities. Count approximately half each of a courgette, pepper and a small leek, 1 tomato and half a clove of garlic per helping.

CHICORY – look for white, well closed heads, with a mere shimmer of green at the tips; choose small to medium rather than big heads, a whole or half per portion respectively. Store in the salad tray of the refrigerator.

LEMONS – the saltiness of the feta should provide most of the bite in this salad. However, let your guests dress it as they like, and put a quarter wedge of a bright yellow fruit on each plate.

OLIVES – small shiny black olives to contrast the whiteness of the feta and chicory – about half a dozen per starter.

FETA – a white Greek cheese, made from goat's, ewe's or cow's milk. It used to come in rectangular rindless blocks, several of which filled a big can similar to those used for olive oil, but nowadays you are more likely to find it in small plastic-wrapped portions. It's important that the cheese is kept moist – usually in brine – and even then you'll find it a little crumbly. Allow 2 oz (50 g) per starter. Keep moist, store refrigerated.

GREEK YOGHURT – better by far, in our opinion, than any other plain yoghurt currently on the market, available in pots of various sizes. Allow about 3½ oz (100 g) per helping.

OLIVE OIL – a little extra virgin oil to dress the starter.

AVORIO RICE – a long-grained Italian variety not to be confused with the short-grained arborio recommended for risottos. 3 oz (75 g or ½ cup) makes 1 portion of pilaf.

SAFFRON – 1 small packet (125 milligrams) is enough for 4 portions of rice, so adjust accordingly.

CHOCOLATE PETIT POTS – for 6 individual petit pots (don't try to make less than 6, you need a little substance when whipping or the recipe will fail) you will need about 6 oz (175 g) chocolate – buy a good cooking variety, packaged or loose; 6 egg yolks; 1 vanilla pod; ½ pint (300 ml) double cream.

OTHER INGREDIENTS – butter for frying the vegetables; extra olive oil for serving the salad.

WINE – you could of course drink Greek with this meal – retsina or white demestica, or a slightly fizzy Cypriot bellapais made by Keo if you can find it. Or, turn if you like to the other end of the Mediterranean for a more complex offering. Penedes, along the coast south-west of Barcelona, is Catalonia's reply to Rioja, with traditional red and white wines made from the same varieties of grapes, though they may be called by different names. However, here, too, things are changing, and from the top, it would seem, for in the late sixties a leading house of the area began to introduce new noble varieties from abroad – cabernet sauvignon, of course, and pinot noir, as well as chardonnay, riesling and gewürztraminer. Miguel Torres' Gran Viña Sol, described as dry white pure and simple on the label, is a blend of chardonnay and the traditional parellada grape. It goes well with this meal except for the dessert – no wine marries with chocolate. Alternatively try Viña Esmeralda from the same house, an intriguing blend of muscat d'Alsace and gewürztraminer, which we found fresh and almost green but deceptively similar to a riesling after a while in the glass.

PREPARATION AND PRECOOKING

Make the petits pots de chocolate the night before if you like, but at least 2 hours in advance of the meal.

Weigh out the chocolate. In a measuring jug measure out a third more water than chocolate; for example 6 oz (175 g) of chocolate requires 8 fl oz (250 ml) of water.

Separate the eggs. Beat the yolks with a whisk or fork until they foam.

Break the chocolate into a heavy saucepan, add the water and vanilla pod, and place over low heat. Whisk until the chocolate has melted into the water and you see a smooth, deeply glistening mix. Whisk in the yolks and continue whisking – the mix must never cook – to the point when the heat makes the consistency thicken. This will happen quickly, so be ready to remove the pan from the heat at once. Continue beating for a minute or so, then work the mixture through a sieve into individual ramekins, wine glasses or small bowls, filling them about three quarters full to leave room for the topping of cream. Chill in the refrigerator.

An hour before your guests are due, whip the cream with a wire or rotary whisk until you see the first pointed peaks. Stop beating, top each little pot of chocolate with whipped cream, and return to the refrigerator.

Wash and with a sharp knife chop the vegetables for the pilaf. Cut the courgettes into strips first, then dice; cut the peppers in half, remove stems, white pith and seeds, cut into long strips and then dice; top and tail the leeks, slice through green ends to check no earth has been trapped there, and cut into thin rounds, about ⅛ inch (3 mm) thick; peel and chop the garlic; scald the tomatoes with boiling water from a kettle, peel, cut in halves, scoop out seeds with a teaspoon and chop finely.

In a frying pan big enough to take the entire pilaf at a depth of 2 inches (5 cm) at most, melt enough butter to cover the bottom well. Add the leeks and garlic and cook gently, stirring until soft – the garlic must not burn or it will turn bitter and spoil the taste. Add the peppers, courgettes and tomatoes and cook for a further 5-8 minutes, until the tomatoes have dissolved more or less. Correct with a little salt and fresh black pepper and set aside.

Take the prawns from the refrigerator, peel and leave in a place just warm enough to lose their chill. Rub your hands with a quarter of a lemon and wash under cold water to get rid of the smell.

Prepare the starters. Chop the root end from the chicory, take off outer leaves and inspect whether inner ones need washing – usually not. Gradually cutting back the root end and breaking off leaves one by one, lay them out on individual plates. Dice the feta and add with the black olives, and complete the display with a quarter chunk of lemon on each plate. Put a little extra virgin oil into a small jug, ready to serve on the side.

Prepare the water for cooking the rice – about 2 pints (1 litre) per cup of rice (2 servings). Add a little salt, cover, and set on the cooker, ready to heat when needed – remember a large quantity of water takes a long time to come to the boil.

COOKING AND PRESENTATION

Have the water for the rice boiling by the time you are ready to sit down to the first course. Pour in the rice, bring back to the boil and reduce to a simmer. Leave the lid off and set the timer for 10 minutes – enough to eat the starter with your guests. Fill a kettle with water and switch to boil, assuming it will switch itself off automatically.

When the 10 minutes are up, switch on the kettle again, strain the rice through a sieve, and pour some boiling water from the kettle over the rice in the sieve. Shake and let drip dry for a moment or two.

Put the pan with the vegetables back over medium heat. In a small bowl dissolve the saffron in a few tablespoons of hot water. Stir the vegetables in the pan, put in the rice, pour the dissolved saffron over it, add a little more butter and the prawns. Stir and heat through until the rice is of an even saffron yellow and dry. Serve immediately, with the Greek yoghurt on the side.

Offer the petits pots last.

TIMBALLO DI MELANZANE

Heinz Bielowski, an Austrian friend, gave us this recipe for a delicious gratin made not only with aubergines, as the name suggests, but some of the best Italian cheeses and tart new apples, too. It's a rich dish you can easily vary and experiment with if you like.

Mortadella; black and green olives

Timballo di melanzane

Salad of black and green grapes

Barolo
Asti Spumante

SHOPPING LIST

MORTADELLA – Bologna is one of the homes of this Italian culinary classic, where we have been offered it as a kind of *amuse geule* before the starter. It is made with ground and larded pork, which is then boiled,; we serve it cut in thick diced chunks with some black and green olives on the side – its smooth texture and rich flavour are irresistible, whatever you put out will be eaten. Make sure you get the genuine Italian variety though, reasonably fresh (there ought to be a date stamp by the manufacturer), and buy a whole piece by eye as regards portions – it won't dry out this way.

CHEESES – fontina, gorgonzola dolce, bel paese and grated parmesan are the kinds called for in Heinz's recipe, given him by a

Modenese chef. Fontina, from the Aosta valley, is of course one of the classics in cheese cookery, but you could substitute appenzeller if necessary. Gorgonzola dolce is not dolcelatte, as some cheese books insist, but a sweeter version of the real article itself. Substitute if necessary with plain gorgonzola rather than dolcelatte, which is an excellent cheese but too creamy here. Bel paese is mild and widely available enough, and so is parmesan, but make sure it is freshly grated, with its aroma still intact.

How much cheese to buy? Quantities depend not only on how many you intend feeding, but the size of your gratin dish, and the equally practical matter that you must be able to slice the cheeses thinly to build up the layers of the gratin – in other words, it's difficult to slice a piece of cheese that is thin already. First choose your ovenproof dish – for example, an enamelled gratin dish, about 2 inches (5 cm) deep, 8 inches (20 cm) long and 5 ½ inches (14 cm) wide will serve 2 generous portions; while a glazed earthenware *lasanghe* dish of similar depth but 13 inches (32.5 cm) long and 10 inches (25 cm) wide will serve 6. Now imagine that with each of the cheeses you are to cover the entire surface of the dish, with a layer about ⅛ inch (3 mm) thick, and you get an idea of the quantities to buy – not all that much in weight, but don't forget that you must have something to slice from, which can always be eaten with another meal. As for the grated parmesan, allow for two layers of similar thickness, plus a little extra to sprinkle over the top. Store the cheeses in the refrigerator – they will be easier to slice if cold.

CRÈME FRAICHE – matured, slightly sour cream, despite the name, but substitute with double cream if you can't find it; mixed half and half with a simple white sauce, ½ pint (300 ml) will be enough to cover a gratin for 6 before it goes into the oven.

BUTTER – for the bottom layer in your gratin dish, plus 1 oz (25 g) or so for the white sauce for 6.

MILK – 1 pint (600 ml) for the white sauce for 6.

FLOUR – 1 oz (25 g) plain white for the white sauce for 6.

NUTMEG – a pinch to season the white sauce, but you could make do without.

AUBERGINES – the recipe calls for 3 layers of them, of the same thickness as the cheeses – ⅛ inch (3 mm).

APPLES – buy enough just for one layer; Bramleys, Cox's or Granny Smiths would be fine.

GRAPES – look around and see whether you can find genuine muscat grapes, green and black ones. Look for waxy yellowish skins, which are a sign of sweetness, and firm black berries with a whitish plume.

OTHER INGREDIENTS – a little olive oil; sugar for sprinkling on the grapes; a little fresh white or brown bread to offer with the main course.

WINES – Barolo is the king of wines and wine of kings, or so the Piedmontese would have it, contradicted by their Tuscan compatriots in favour of their own king, Brunello di Montalcino – a dispute we feel no need to enter, for the wines can be outstanding and distinct enough not to tangle. There is one similarity, though: both need considerable age in bottle, yet to buy an old Barolo may be only part of the solution, for in Piedmont, too, changes are afoot. Old-style Barolo from the classic nebbiolo grape was crushed green stalks and all, and matured far too long in tannin-laden oak, so that only the best vintages recovered after years and years in bottle – that's what you may find in ancient bottles still not ready to drink, while those on supermarket shelves invariably are hopelessly young. What to buy then, unless you have the guidance of a merchant with a list of Barolos that tells he is taking an interest in them, Adnams of Southwold, for example? We rang the Italian Trade Centre, who suggested we ask Paul Merritt, of Alivini, and hence the wines with this menu. But, apart from his advice, Mr Merritt gave us a copy of *Life Beyond Lambrusco* by Nicolas Belfrage, Master of Wine (Sidgwick & Jackson, 1985) – an extraordinary thing for an importer of food and wine to do you might think. It's an eye-opener of a book, based on a wealth of detail, yet compelling, indeed full of life. Read it if you want to boost your enjoyment of Italian wines and buy them at their still under-rated best. Here are the wines we tried and liked – 1980 Barolo, Casa Vinicola Fratelli Oddero; 1980 Barolo, Casa Vinicola Franco Fiorina; 1985 Asti Spumante, Villa Banfi.

GRAPPA – a clear eau-de-vie distilled from grape lees all over Italy, but those from the Trentino – made by Roberto Zeni, for example – are especially good. It's an acquired taste, strong and scented enough to ask only for a teaspoon or two in the grape salad. (If the purchase of a whole bottle strikes you as extravagant, and the grapes are good, why not eat them as they come? Grappa finds its uses, though – in a cup of strong black coffee on a cold winter's day, for example.)

PREPARATION AND PRECOOKING

Some 2 hours before the appointed time, preheat the grill.

Meanwhile wash the aubergines, slice them into discs no thicker than ⅛ inch (3 mm), which is the standard thickness for all layers in this recipe, brush with olive oil, and grill under high heat for 2 minutes each side. Take out the grid, set it aside with the slices on, and let them cool.

In a heavy saucepan melt 1 oz (25 g) of butter over lowish heat, until it foams. Stir in the same amount of white flour and cook for 3 minutes. Pour in the milk and whisk to make the mix smooth. Increase the heat as you continue whisking, until the sauce comes to the boil. Whisk in a mere pinch of salt, reduce the heat and simmer for 45 minutes or so, stirring every now and then, while you continue with the rest of your preparations.

Wash the apples, peel, and slice vertically, discarding cores.

Cover the bottom of the gratin dish with a generous layer of butter.

Slice the fontina with a cheese wire if you have one, or improvise with a piece of dental floss, but don't attempt to slice your cheeses with a knife – even a cheese knife with a special non-stick blade will stick and squash bigger slices than the thinness called for here, of the softer cheeses especially.

Lay the fontina slices in the gratin dish, and cover with a layer of grilled aubergine slices.

Slice the gorgonzola dolce and lay in the dish. Put in a layer of apples, and cover them with a layer of grated parmesan. Put another layer of grilled aubergine slices on top.

Slice the bel paese and lay in the dish. Add the third and final layer of aubergine slices, and cover with another layer of grated parmesan.

Finish the white sauce by straining it through a sieve into another saucepan, over low heat. This may take a few minutes if the sieve is fine – use a cooking spoon or spatula to push the sauce through. Whisk in the crème fraiche or double cream, season with a little fresh black pepper and a pinch, no more, of finely grated nutmeg, and pour over the top of the gratin to make a generous, even cover. Sprinkle with a little extra grated parmesan and set aside, ready for the oven – a gratin for 6 of the thickness described will need about 30 minutes in an oven preheated to gas ¼/240°F/130°C.

Wash the grapes, shake off water, destalk and slice with a sharp knife. Remove the pips if they bother you. Put the cut grapes in a glass bowl, sprinkle them with a little sugar if not naturally sweet enough, add a mere teaspoon or two of grappa, toss gently and refrigerate.

Last, peel and cut the mortadella, first into ½ inch (1 cm) and then into dice. Put them on a big plate with the green and black olives.

COOKING AND PRESENTATION

Assuming you will want to begin eating about half an hour from the time your guests arrive, put the gratin into the preheated cool oven as soon as your party is complete.

Offer the mortadella with olives.

Serve the gratin in the dish you cooked it in, portioning it out at table. Offer white and/or brown bread with it.

Offer the grape salad and Asti Spumante.

THANKSGIVING

Few dishes can be more comforting than a good chowder, whether it contains fish or clams or not. You could also prepare this near-vegetarian version for a simple lunch if you like, with some delicious indigenous materials added for good measure.

Sweet corn chowder

York ham; cos lettuce with mustard dressing

Cheddar and new Cox's of the season

Biddenden dry cider and/or Müller-Thurgau

SHOPPING LIST

CORN CHOWDER – for 4 helpings you will need 2 ears of corn on the cob, well closed with all the husks in place; 4 medium potatoes; 1 medium onion; 2 rashers of streaky bacon; 1½ oz (40 g) butter; 1 bay leaf; ¾ pint (450 ml) milk; salt and pepper.

YORK HAM – "Yorkshire is famous for Hams; and the Reason is this: Their Salt is much finer than ours in London, it is a large clear Salt, and gives the Meat a fine Flavour." Thus Hannah Glasse in *The Art of Cookery, made Plain and Easy*, 1747 – too easy an explanation, perhaps. However, York hams are still the best unless you prefer Bradenham ones, which are cured in molasses rather than salt. Buy the ham cooked, on the bone. Sue Cloke, of Paxton & Whitfield, advised us to look for a good overall shape, with bright orange breadcrumbs on the outside, an even white layer of fat all round and moist marbled meat of a delicate pink. Watch the meat being sliced off the bone with a knife – its own bone, not something stuck through on the carving stand – judging by eye how much you need per portion. Eat it on the day you buy for maximum taste and moisture. Store well wrapped in the refrigerator until serving.

CHEDDAR – unpasteurised traditional farmhouse cheddar can be found in specialist shops, in small clothbound truckles of a few pounds if you are lucky, which make attractive gifts as well. Patrick Rance (*The Great British Cheese Book*, Papermac, 1983) writes of the varied character of cheddar, sweet and sharp, moist and hard, different from farm to farm, season to season, cheesemaker to cheesemaker. So taste before you buy, and buy from more than one cheese if you can. Store in a cool place.

COS LETTUCE – or indeed anything crisp and green you fancy, provided it will stand up to a mustard dressing; white chicory and buttery young fennel bulbs might be alternatives or additions. Store in the salad tray of the refrigerator.

COX'S ORANGE PIPPINS – we're aware that the number of apple varieties brought to market nowadays represents but a lamentably small part of what may be grown privately, but wonder whether there can be another type of apple to surpass the aroma and texture of this 19th-century English cross when in prime condition. Buy them direct from an orchard if you can, as the new harvest is picked at the end of September and on. Buy lots, and store them in perforated plastic bags in a cold place. Don't worry if you see signs of condensation inside the bags, as a little moisture helps to preserve the apples.

FOR THE MUSTARD DRESSING – mustard powder, or Dijon or Meaux mustard ready-mixed, plus an oil with a strong nutty flavour, walnut or hazelnut. Make sure the oil is still fresh, and keep it refrigerated.

OTHER INGREDIENTS – bread and butter to serve on the side with the chowder and ham; buy crusty white and wholemeal or rye.

CIDER AND/OR WINE – consider drinking cider with a meal of this kind. Biddenden Vineyards in Kent, whose prize-winning ortega wine we mentioned in Menu 1, make the best cider we have ever tasted – brilliant yet full of fruit, dry, with the unmistakable touch of the master winemaker. Or, try it as a surprise aperitif if you think your guests might feel short-changed unless given wine. What then, if serving a wine? Salt ham and salad with a mustard dressing are difficult companions for any wine, as are apples, though not cheese, as an old adage of the wine trade says: "Buy on an apple, sell on cheese." A grapey white, with a little spice and a hint of sweetness, might take you through this meal, and you may well find it among English wines – a fresh Müller-Thurgau, for example; alternatively try a French Vouvray or Montlouis, made from the chenin blanc grape.

PREPARATION AND PRECOOKING

Chill the cider and/or wines.

Make the chowder a few hours in advance if you like, so that you will only need to reheat it.

Pull the husks off the corn on the cob, and with a knife or fingers push down the length of each ear, removing the corn. Wash the potatoes, peel and dice – about ¼ inch (6 mm) per side; peel the onion and chop fine; chop the streaky bacon into tiny squares.

In a saucepan voluminous enough to hold the chowder, melt ½ oz (15 g) of the butter, add the bacon and cook for 2 minutes. Add the diced onion and continue until it is soft. Add the potatoes, ¾ pint (450 ml) water and 1 bay leaf, and cook for 10 minutes on medium to high heat.

Add the corn and milk, bring back to a little less than a boil, and simmer for a further 5 minutes. Remove the bay leaf. Stir in 1 oz (25 g) of the butter, season with a little salt and a generous amount of fresh black pepper, and serve or set aside, lid on, to reheat later.

Cut the root end from the cos lettuce and discard outer leaves. Cut a little more from the root end and unfold, rinsing leaves only if necessary. Shake dry, dab with kitchen paper, and set aside in a cool place.

Make the mustard dressing. In a mixing bowl whisk your oil into the mustard, drop for drop at first if you are using powder, a little faster if it's ready-mixed, until you get a smooth sauce. Set aside to mature in a cool place.

Wash and dry the apples, and arrange with the cheese on a platter.

COOKING AND PRESENTATION

Reheat the soup if not served fresh, and offer in big bowls or plates with bread and butter on the side.

Serve the ham portioned out on individual plates. Give the mustard dressing another whisk, and toss the salad at table, breaking the lettuce leaves by hand first.

Last, offer the cheese and apples.

ANTIPASTO AND PASTA

A short version of a full-blown Tuscan meal,
big enough all the same, but with short cuts
built in – you can buy the components for the
starter almost ready-made.

Fett'unta, with dried tomatoes in extra virgin oil

Tagliatelle with mozzarella

Pears and pecorino

Chianti Classico

SHOPPING LIST

BREAD – for the fett'unta, literally 'oiled slice', made with toasted
Tuscan bread, garlic, and olive oil. We bake our own version of
this unsalted white bread, but any fresh white loaf of good
quality will do. Count 2 chunky slices per head.

TAGLIATELLE – buy fresh if you can, green, white or mixed – 4-6
oz (125-175 g) per head. Carry home carefully – without putting
other things on top – and store in the refrigerator.

DRIED TOMATOES – Carapelli of Florence export this simple
delicacy in small glass jars that may seem a little pricy but aren't
because the contents go far enough. Allow a couple of pieces per
person.

OLIVE OIL – only *extra vergine* will do, from Tuscany if possible.
Look for a greenish rather than yellow oil for this dish, pressed

from early rather than late picked olives, which have a slight sharpness all of their own. You won't need all that much – a tablespoon per slice of fett'unta perhaps.

TOMATOES – for the pasta sauce, and entirely different in flavour from the dried variety described above. Buy them in cans, peeled or chopped, or creamed in packets. A 1 lb (500 g) packet or a 14 oz (397 g) can will make enough sauce for 4.

ONION – 1 medium onion will provide the base of a tomato sauce for 4.

GARLIC – 1 clove per slice of fett'unta, plus some more for the tomato sauce – 2 cloves for 4 portions.

HERBS – fresh parsley, oregano and thyme would go well with the sauce, but dried mixed herbs will do.

BASIL – get it fresh if you can, a little plant or package, to sprinkle over the pasta when serving.

PEARS – what the Tuscans traditionally like to eat with their pecorino, so look around for what is on offer – Conference, Williams, la Belle Hélène. Whatever you buy, make sure the pears smell sweet or they won't be ripe. On the other hand, reject fruit with bruised or discoloured skins, and handle with care. Buy 1 per head.

MOZZARELLA – don't be misled into buying the cooking variety for this dish. Get the eating kind, available moist, in small balls wrapped in paper or plastic. You need not spend the extra money for the more expensive buffalo milk variety – freshness is the most important factor. Allow half a mozzarella for each helping of pasta. Store, half submerged in water, in the refrigerator for no more than a day.

PECORINO – sheep cheese, as the name says. Usually crumbly and moist when young, it grows considerably harder and spicier with age. Don't despair if you can't find anything beyond the standard romano or sardo types that are more suitable for cooking; see if you can find English sheep cheeses instead. We recently tried a Mendip, a well made soft cheese with both spice and cream. Buy by taste and eye.

WINE – what better wine than Chianti, you might ask, to go with simple Tuscan food? But in Tuscany, too, things are changing, not least because of the regulations first laid down by the Iron Baron, Bettino Ricasoli of Brolio, and reconfirmed in essence by the denominazione di origine controllata laws of 1963. Sangiovese is the main grape, and excellent it is, but white grapes, too, are prescribed for the mix to such an extent that the easily grown but indifferent trebbiano may still spoil the wine. Clearly the law must be changed, and before it's too late, for not a few of the leading houses have long set off on their own ways, making wines that, quite apart from being good, have helped to push Chianti into a corner. A recent blind tasting of Tuscan reds by WINE magazine proves that single grape wines may be best. Brunello di Montalcino, made from sangiovese grosso alone, swept the board, as no more than two Chiantis were judged in the top three-star group, and only one of them from the Classico region – 1981 Riserva Villa Antinori; while the other was a Chianti Rufina – 1979 Riserva Castello di Nipozzano. Try those two and compare – there are those who hold that Rufina (not to be confused with Ruffino, an old-established grower and producer of Pontassieve in that region) makes the better wines.

PREPARATION

There is little you can prepare in advance of this meal, except for the tomato sauce which can be made even on the night before. Peel the onion or onions and chop, together with 2 cloves of garlic per onion. In a heavy saucepan heat a little olive oil, add the onion and garlic and cook gently, taking care not to burn the garlic – it will go bitter if you do. Add the puréed or chopped tomatoes, herbs and a little salt, and cook for about 20 minutes over medium heat. Sieve the sauce and cook it for a little longer if still thin, then set aside.

A quarter of an hour before your guests are due fill a saucepan big enough to cook the tagliatelle with water – 1 gallon (4.5 litres) per 4 portions – add salt, cover, bring to the boil, then switch off and leave standing by.

Peel enough cloves of garlic for the fett'unta – 1 per slice or 2 per portion; then halve the cloves lengthwise.

Take the mozzarella from the refrigerator, unwrap, and with a sharp wet knife cut into ½ inch (1 cm) dice; set aside. Take the tagliatelle, too, from the refrigerator and let them warm to room temperature.

Last, pick 2-3 basil leaves per head, chop roughly and set aside, ready to sprinkle over the pasta as you serve it.

COOKING AND PRESENTATION

Preheat the grill to high heat as your guests are enjoying their second aperitifs. Slice the bread for the fett'unta, 1 inch (2.5 cm) thick, counting 2 slices per person unless they are very small, in which case increase the number; and in a small saucepan warm but don't heat some extra virgin oil – about 1 tablespoon per slice of bread.

When the grill is hot, quickly grill the bread on both sides until golden brown outside but still soft within. Rub with half a clove of garlic per side, sprinkle with a little coarse salt, pour the warm oil over them and serve immediately, with the dried tomatoes and fresh black pepper on the side.

Bring the pasta water to the boil. Gently reheat the tomato sauce – it should be warm rather than hot – put in the diced mozzarella, and leave standing by. When the water is boiling fast, drop in the tagliatelle, stir, and watch them come back to the surface after 3 minutes or so. Try one – it should be cooked, with a little resistance left to the bite. Drain through a colander, shake, let drip for a moment, then portion out on individual plates. Pour the warm tomato and mozzarella sauce on top, sprinkle over the basil and serve immediately.

Offer the pears and pecorino last.

WINTER

DINNER FOR TWO, FOUR, SIX, EIGHT

Ideal for a birthday or celebratory dinner
when there isn't much time for preparation,
here is a simple yet delicate menu, none too
obvious in components either.

Salad of palm hearts and avocado

Fillets of John Dory, cooked on a bed of vegetables

Syllabub; almond macaroons

Champagne

SHOPPING LIST

JOHN DORY – or St Peter's fish, as it is known in Mediterranean
countries as well as Scandinavia, allegedly because of the single
black spot or finger print the saint left on either side of the flat but
upright body and head. It is not always available, so find out
what your chances are and order what you will need if possible;
a flat fish, such as lemon sole or brill, might be an alternative.
Because of its relatively big head, the weight of a John Dory is
not a good indicator of how much meat you are actually buying.
Think in terms of fillets, which, because of its compressed
shape, are easy to visualize – a really big specimen should
provide 4 fillets of a size sufficient for 1 portion each. Have the
fish filleted if you are going to cook it more or less as you get it
home; otherwise have it gutted only and do the filleting yourself
– it's easily done, and described in the preparations. Unwrap the

fish when you get it home, but beware of the spikes in the fins and around the body. Cover it loosely and refrigerate.

PALM HEARTS – a number of canned brands are on the market, from Brazil and other tropical countries. You won't need much per starter – 2-3 sticks to balance half an avocado.

AVOCADO – count half a pear per head, but do make sure it is ripe (yet not over-ripe) and has flavour too – there is not enough in such a simple salad to let you disguise its absence. Wrinkly dark Hass is a variety we like for its nutty taste. Buy what you need plus one extra to try a day in advance if you want to make sure everything will be all right.

VEGETABLES – carrots, sweet peppers and courgettes – the idea is to make a bed of vegetables on which to cook the fish. Buy a handful of the smallest carrots you can find, half a green, yellow or red pepper and a couple of courgettes per helping.

LEMON – 1 per 4 starters; plus 1 to make a syllabub for 4-6.

DOUBLE CREAM – ½ pint (300 ml) will make 4 generous helpings of syllabub, for which quantity you will also need ¼ pint (150 ml) good dry sherry and 3 tablespoons of three-star cognac or better (never use so-called cooking brands – their tired flavours will show through), and 2 oz (50 g) of caster sugar.

OTHER INGREDIENTS – a good knob or two of butter to cook the vegetables and fish, unsalted or slightly salted and as fresh as you can get; extra virgin olive oil for the salad.

ALMOND MACAROONS – Amaretti di Saronno, individually wrapped in colourful rice papers, are our favourite make, available in old-fashioned red cans of various sizes. Allow 3 per person.

CHAMPAGNE – don't undermine your food with a substitute for the sake of a little extra money, but don't be misled into thinking that price or *grande marque* are guarantees for a bottle you will enjoy. Even supermarket champagnes have won professional tastings recently, with unfortunate consequences as we found out. A sudden increase in demand had depleted the stocks of the well publicised winner, and a different maker's wine appeared on those same shelves, behind the same label, by the time we got to try it . . . However, if you don't know a merchant who quaffs bubbly regularly and could thus advise you on the spot, here are four houses whose usually competitively priced non-vintage wines have yet to disappoint us – Heidsieck Monopole, Laurent Perrier, Pol Roger and Taittinger. Whatever you buy, make sure the label shows that your choice is dry – brut or even extra brut – for the odd bottle of old-fashioned medium *gout francais* is found here.

PREPARATION

Make the syllabub long enough in advance to chill it in the refrigerator, the night before if you like – provided the mix is well made, it will keep without separating.

Grate the rind of a whole lemon and set aside. Cut the lemon in half, squeeze, and strain the juice into a mixing bowl big enough to whip the syllabub in. Add the dry sherry and brandy, add the sugar and stir until it has dissolved. Add the cream and whisk with a wire whisk or rotary beater until it thickens, standing in soft peaks. Don't attempt to use a mixer for a syllabub and don't overbeat. Spoon it into wine glasses and refrigerate for 3 hours at least.

An hour before the meal take the fish from the refrigerator and put the champagne in to chill.

Wash and peel the carrots unless very small. Wash the peppers and courgettes. With a sharp knife cut the carrots in long quarters, removing hard cores. Cut again lengthwise, and across, until you have sticks double the length and thickness of matchsticks.

Cut the peppers in half, remove stems, white membranes and

seeds and cut into long strips, approximately similar in size to the carrot sticks.

Top and tail the courgettes and slice lengthwise to make sticks similar to the carrots and peppers. Salt the courgettes lightly and set aside in a colander.

Open the can of palm hearts and drain. Portion out the sticks on to individual plates, and sprinkle lightly with lemon juice.

With a sharp stainless steel knife cut the avocados in half, discard stones, and pull off skins. Immediately sprinkle with lemon juice, rubbing it over the surfaces gently to prevent browning. Lay the halves, cavity down, and slice carefully lengthwise. Sprinkle the new cuts with lemon juice and arrange the slices among the palm heart pieces. Set aside in a cool place.

Fillet the fish unless this has been done for you already. Lay it on a board, and with a pointed sharp knife make a cut just inside the spikes at the edge of the body. Push the knife right through the bones, working round the fish, removing the spiky edges. Slash the skin across the root of the tail, and lift and pull it off towards the head. Cut off the head. Make an incision along the line of the backbone. Slide the blade of the knife inside, flatten it towards the outside of the body, and loosen first one fillet, then the other three. Put the clean fillets aside, wipe the board, re-sharpen your knife so that it cuts like a razor and slice the flesh across, against the grain, into strips about ⅙ inch (4 mm) thick. Put the strips aside, wipe your hands with a quarter lemon and rinse under cold water – hot water opens the pores, and the oil of the fish will get caught in them.

COOKING AND PRESENTATION

In a shallow saucepan, or a frying pan with a lid, melt a knob or two of butter over low heat. Put in the vegetables, salt and pepper lightly, and let them stew very slowly, lid on, while you eat the first course.

Sprinkle the salad with a little extra virgin olive oil, salt, fresh black pepper, and serve.

Stir a little more butter into the vegetables when they are almost done, increase the heat and distribute them evenly over the pan. Quickly lay the slices of John Dory on top, salt and pepper lightly, and replace the lid for 3 minutes. Test a piece of the fish – it should be opaque and just done. Serve immediately from the pan, pouring pan juices over each portion.

Serve the syllabub, almond macaroons and more champagne. You can play hot-air balloons with the rice papers that Amaretti di Saronno come in – unwrap a double macaroon, shake the paper, straighten it and roll into a tall hollow cylinder, not too tight, about as thick as a thumb. Stand the cylinder in a clean ash tray and light its top. Watch the flame burn to the very bottom – at the last moment, suddenly the charred cylinder will take off, rising as high as the ceiling if you're lucky.

A MEXICAN MEAL

We spent winter in Chiapas, in the very
south of Mexico, one year, Gerd pounding
away on an old Royal typewriter not a few
years his senior, Liz pottering around markets
and learning to cook a variety of dishes from
Indians and long-resident North Americans.
Here are some of the recipes she brought
back – most of them can be prepared in
advance. Serve them together for a convivial
feast.

Guacamole

Josefa's Mexican rice

Jo Bordages' beans

Chayotes, Vera Cruz style

Raw sauce

Bowls of grated cheese and chopped onion

*Fresh fruit and nuts – oranges and other citrus
fruit, fresh dates and nuts*

Zinfandel

All quantities are for 6 generous helpings.
Use as given here or in proportion.

SHOPPING LIST

GUACAMOLE – for this simple but authentic version you will need 3 ripe avocados, of the wrinkled black variety if you can find them; 1 teaspoon lime or lemon juice; 1-2 tablespoons finely chopped onion; 1 clove of garlic, peeled and finely chopped; about 3 tablespoons olive oil; salt and pepper.

JOSEFA'S MEXICAN RICE – you will need 3 ripe tomatoes; 2 medium courgettes or 4 oz (125 g) French beans; 3 small carrots; 1 ½ tablespoons each of chopped onion and olive oil; 2 cloves of garlic; 1 ½ cups Italian avorio or Uncle Ben's rice; 1 chicken stock cube.

JO BORDAGES' BEANS – you will need 1 lb (500 g) dried red kidney beans, preferably from the most recent harvest; 1 chicken stock cube; 1 peeled onion spiked with 5 cloves; 1 tablespoon cumin seeds; 10 dried chilies; salt.

CHAYOTES, VERA CRUZ STYLE – you will need 3 chayotes (a kind of squash, pale green and about the size of avocados, found in most Indian stores); 4 ripe tomatoes; 2 onions; 2 tablespoons finely chopped parsley; 1 fresh or dried chili; 10 stoned green olives; 3 tablespoons olive oil.

RAW SAUCE – you will need 2 ripe tomatoes; ½ medium onion; 1 clove of garlic; 2 sprigs of fresh coriander, or parsley if you can't find or don't like coriander; 1 fresh or dried chili; salt and pepper.

CHEESE – cheddar or a mild young caerphilly, 4 oz (125 g) to serve grated.

ONIONS – peeled and finely chopped to serve as a garnish.

WINE – we did drink indigenous wines in Mexico, some of which were pleasant enough, but no one here imports them, so why not go north and try a zinfandel, the Californian speciality, with this meal? Made from grapes of the same name, it can be spicy and dark, reaching considerable age, finesse and price.

There are lighter and even *blush* – i.e. pink – zinfandels, though, reminiscent of beaujolais almost. Try Ridge Vineyards, Fetzer or Heitz, but ask if you choose a more expensive wine whether it is ready to drink.

PREPARATION AND PRECOOKING

Jo Bordages' beans can be made one or even two days in advance. Soak the beans overnight in cold water or cover with boiling water and leave for 2 hours. When they have recovered most of the moisture lost in drying, put the beans in a saucepan, cover with cold unsalted water, add 1 chicken stock cube, 1 peeled onion spiked with 5 cloves, 1 tablespoon of cumin and 10 dried chiles. Bring to the boil and boil for 10 minutes, then reduce the heat and simmer until cooked – probably about 40 minutes, there should be some bite left. Test and add a little salt if necessary. Drain through a colander but reserve a little of the liquid to keep with the beans, then set aside to cool. Store, covered, in a cool place.

Precook the chayotes – put them whole in a saucepan, cover with water, bring to the boil, then reduce the heat and simmer for 45 minutes. Test with a skewer. When they are soft, drain the chayotes and set them aside.

Josefa's rice, too, can be made in advance – perhaps while the chayotes are simmering. Bring some water to the boil in a kettle and pour over the 3 tomatoes, to scald and blister their skins. Peel, cut in halves and scoop out seeds with a spoon. Discard seeds and chop finely. Add 2 tomatoes to this process if you are also about to make the raw sauce, as described below. Plus a further 4 if you are going to finish off the chayotes as well.

Wash the courgettes and carrots for the rice, top and tail, and slice thinly. Peel an onion and chop very finely – you will need no more than 1½ tablespoons for the rice, but 1-2 more for the guacamole, and ½ chopped onion for the raw sauce. Peel 2 cloves of garlic and chop finely.

Bring a little more water to the boil in the kettle, then set aside, ready to come back to the boil more or less instantly.

In a frying pan with a lid heat the olive oil over medium heat. Add the rice, chopped onion and garlic, and stir until the rice begins to brown, but be careful not to burn the garlic or it will taste bitter. Add the carrots, courgettes and tomatoes and stir for 1 minute. Heat the kettle again and add boiling water, almost to the brim of the pan. Add the stock cube and stir to dissolve. Adjust the heat to a mere simmer and cover; leave the lid on for 23 minutes. Lift it and see whether any liquid is left. If there is, replace the lid for 2 more minutes or so. Serve immediately or leave until required – overnight, covered in a cool place, if necessary – the rice can be reheated by adding a touch more oil and stirring a little until warmed through.

Make the raw sauce no more than 2 hours in advance. Peel the 2 tomatoes as described already, deseed and chop finely, together with the ½ onion, 1 clove of garlic, 2 sprigs of coriander or parsley, and 1 chili. Add 1 teaspoon of salt and mix well.

Make the guacamole last in your preparations, no more than 1 hour in advance. Cut the 3 avocados in half, discard stones, and scoop out the flesh with a spoon into a mixing bowl. Add the 1 tablespoon lime or lemon juice and mash. Add the 2 tablespoons chopped onion, 1 clove of chopped garlic, approximately 3 tablespoons of olive oil, a little salt and fresh black pepper, and mix. Transfer to a serving bowl, cover and refrigerate.

Last, grate the cheese coarsely, so that you can pick it up with your fingers to distribute it over the beans or rice, as you like.

COOKING AND PRESENTATION

All the dishes should be offered more or less at the same time, so reheat the beans in their liquid and the Mexican rice slowly, while you finish the chayotes.

Peel the cooked chayotes and dice into 1 inch (2.5 cm) pieces. Heat the 3 tablespoons olive oil in a saucepan, add 1 clove of finely chopped garlic, and cook until it begins to change colour. Add the 2 finely chopped onions, the 4 peeled, deseeded and finely chopped tomatoes, the 2 tablespoons finely chopped coriander or parsley, the diced chayotes and the diced chili if dried. Stir, cover, and cook over low heat for 10 minutes. Add the 10 stoned green olives and the fresh chili as you are about to serve the dish.

Offer the guacamole, grated cheese, chopped raw onion and raw sauce in separate bowls, together with the three warm dishes.

Serve fresh fruit and nuts at the end.

FROM OLD AUSTRIA

Don't let the long names put you off this menu, it's perfectly straightforward and quickly prepared. You need a big frying pan or two, and guests who appreciate food more or less straight from the fire.

South Tirolean wine soup

Wiener schnitzel; cucumber salad

Kaiserschmarrn – emperor's pancakes

Wines from South Tirol

SHOPPING LIST

WINE SOUP – for 4 generous helpings you will need 1 pt (600 ml) good quality beef consommé ; 5 egg yolks; ½ pint (300 ml) good quality dry white wine, South Tirolean chardonnay if possible; ½ pint (300 ml) double cream; 2 stale white rolls; 1 oz (25 g) butter; a little grated cinnamon.

VEAL – for the Wiener schnitzel – order in advance from your butcher if you are not sure he has veal all the time; ask for 1 biggish escalope from the cushion or topside per portion – i.e. about two palms big – and cut so that the meat will be approximately ⅙ inch (4 mm) thick once it has been beaten lightly.

OTHER INGREDIENTS FOR THE SCHNITZEL – to cook 4 you will also need 2 eggs; a little milk or water; 2 oz (50 g) plain white flour; 3 oz (75 g) white breadcrumbs; 6-7 oz (175-200 g) lard. Double the quantity of lard if you want to cook in two pans at a time, and have a little extra in store, just in case the fat turns brown; please note that the fat must be used once only.

LEMONS – a quarter of an attractive bright fruit per schnitzel.

CUCUMBER – 1 large one, firm, round, without cuts or bruises, will make salad for 4.

PAPRIKA – a good pinch or two for the salad, provided it is freshly ground; substitute black pepper otherwise.

KAISERSCHMARRN – originally a simple alpine pancake, shredded in the pan, fit for an emperor nonetheless. For 4 helpings of the not inconsiderable size you would expect in Austria you will need 3 oz (75 g) sultanas; 3 tablespoons Hungarian apricot barack or three-star cognac; 8 eggs; 3 fl oz (75 ml) milk; about 2 oz (50 g) icing sugar; 6 oz (175 g) plain white flour; a pinch of salt; 3 oz (75 g) unsalted butter.

OTHER INGREDIENTS – olive oil and wine vinegar for the salad.

WINES – if you begin with wine in your soup, maybe it's best not to drink any more with it, lest you overpower the flavour. Try a glass or two of Goldmuskateller as an aperitif and return to it with the Kaiserschmarrn at the end, if you like, unless you change to a Rosenmuskateller then. Here are four of our favourites, all of them made and bottled by Herbert Tiefenbrunner, at Schloss Turmhof – 1984 Goldmuskateller; their ordinary 1984 Chardonnay; 1984 Chardonnay 'made and matured from specially selected grapes fermented and matured for six months in new 225 litre oak casks' as the label says; and 1983 Rosenmuskateller, a pink, perfumed, disconcertingly dry wine.

PREPARATION AND PRECOOKING

A few hours in advance, even on the night before if you can, preheat a small mixing bowl with hot water while you sort through the sultanas. Divide fruits that stick together and remove the stems. Warm the brandy. Pour the hot water away and mix the sultanas and brandy in the bowl. Cover and set aside in a warm place.

An hour before the appointed time, take the veal from the refrigerator, unwrap and lay on a board. With a sharp knife remove pieces of fat or other non-meat tissue; at intervals of 2 inches (5 cm) or so make small incisions in the thin membrane you may find around the edges, to prevent the meat buckling under heat; leave the escalopes on one side to warm to room temperature.

Measure out the wine for the soup, but chill the rest.

Make the basic batter for the Kaiserschmarrn. Separate the eggs – yolks into one mixing bowl, whites into another – and set aside. Measure out the milk and flour. Stir the yolks, adding a pinch of salt and a little flour, so that you get a smooth paste without lumps. Add a little of the milk, stir or whisk, and continue stirring until you have used up these two ingredients and the basic batter drops in a continuous stream if poured from a spoon. If you get lumps, take a sieve and another bowl and quickly work the lumpy batter through the sieve. Set the batter aside in a cool place.

Beat the egg whites with a wire or electric rotary whisk until you get pointed peaks, and set aside.

Prepare the croûtons for the soup. Dice the rolls with a sharp knife, removing crusts as you go – about ⅓ inch (8 mm) per side or so. In a frying pan melt the butter over medium to high heat, add the diced bread, and fry until golden brown. Sprinkle the finished croûtons with a little cinnamon, and leave them on a double layer of kitchen paper to absorb surplus fat.

Wash the cucumber, peel and slice on a mandolin, or cut as thin as you can with a knife, leaving seeds in place. Salt slightly and let drip in a colander in a cool place.

Prepare for cooking the Wiener schnitzel – break the eggs into a soup plate or similar dish, big enough to let you dunk in one escalope at a time; add a few drops of milk or water and beat with a fork until the yolks and whites have merged. On a board or similar flat surface spread flour for dusting the meat, on another spread the breadcrumbs; weigh out the lard and put it in a big frying pan or two – the schnitzel must not overlap and should be able to swim quite freely once placed in the hot fat in the pan.

COOKING AND PRESENTATION

Make the soup so that you can serve it from the saucepan, just as soon as it is ready. Warm the soup plates in the oven if you like.

Pour the consommé into a saucepan and heat gently. Separate the eggs – you need the yolks, not the whites, for this recipe. Beating steadily with a wire whisk, add the white wine and cream to the hot consommé, then the egg yolks. Pour into individual plates or bowls just as soon as the ingredients have combined and the soup is creamy. Distribute the croûtons, sprinkle a little extra cinnamon on top and serve without delay.

Preheat the oven to gas 4/350°F/180°C if you are going to fry more Wiener schnitzel than you can serve straight from the pan.

Finish the cucumber salad. Shake the colander to remove excess liquid and turn into a salad or serving bowl. Don't worry if the water content still seems high – the Austrians eat it that way, refreshing and cool. Toss with a little wine vinegar, olive oil, and paprika or fresh black pepper.

Over medium heat, melt the lard for frying the schnitzel, about the thickness of a thumb deep at least; don't let it begin to smoke and burn.

Salt the escalopes on both sides, lay them on the flour, turn and shake lightly – only a thin layer of flour should remain. Dunk the dusted escalopes in the beaten egg, let drip, put them down on the breadcrumbs and turn, without pressure. Shake, so that only a thin, lightly attached layer of crumbs remains, and cook without delay – the schnitzel will turn out soggy if you stop at this stage, which is why breading is not part of the preparation in these instructions.

Test the temperature of the fat by holding a fork under running cold water and drawing it through the pan – the fat is ready if you hear an angry hiss.

Put the escalopes into the pan or pans, one or two at a time, provided they can swim freely and don't overlap. Turn the heat up as the fat drops temporarily in temperature, and fry until the underside is golden brown – after 1½ minutes or so. Shake the pan repeatedly during this time, so that the fat also runs over the top of the schnitzel and the coat of flour, egg and breadcrumbs begins to lift, but keep an eye on the temperature – the fat must not smoke. Turn the meat and cook for another 1½ minutes or so, shaking the pan as described, until the second side, too, is an even golden brown.

Lift the done schnitzel from the pan, place on a double layer of kitchen paper to absorb some of the excess fat, turn, and serve without delay. Place a quarter lemon on each plate – in Vienna each guest would squeeze his own over the breadcrumbs, according to his or her taste. Offer the cucumber salad on the side.

If you have to fry more schnitzel than you can do at a time, put them in the preheated oven for a moment or two, no more. In any case, leave the oven on gas ¼/240°F/130°C for the last course, and put in a platter to serve the Kaiserschmarrn on.

It's better if the guests wait for the Schmarrn than the Schmarrn for the guests, goes an old Austrian saying, but don't worry, it takes hardly any time at all to cook this simplest of sweets.

Give the batter another stir, then fold in the beaten egg whites and sultanas soaked in brandy. Put a generous knob of butter in a frying pan and place over medium to high heat. When the butter is turning brown, pour in part of the batter – about the thickness of a little finger deep; turn the pancake after 2 minutes or so, when the underside should be golden brown. Cook for 1 more minute, tear with two forks into pieces about 1 inch (2.5 cm) square, put on the serving platter in the oven, melt some more butter in the pan, and continue until all the batter is used up. Let the last batch, too, rest in the oven for a minute or two, then sprinkle the lot with a little of the icing sugar and serve with extra sugar on the side.

EAST BY SOUTH

Vegetarian, from southern Europe and the Middle East, with plenty of flavour and not without substance. You will need a small piece of muslin to strain the soaked funghi.

Aubergine fritters

Barley with funghi porcini

Fresh date and banana pudding

Bulgarian wine

SHOPPING LIST

AUBERGINES – eggplants or *melanzane;* a large one will serve 2-3, depending on just how big it is. Aubergines transport well thanks to their tough skins and high moisture content, but look at them nevertheless, rejecting bruised or otherwise misshapen specimens.

GARLIC – 1 clove per aubergine.

SPANISH ONION – allow 1 large onion per 4 portions or pound (500 g) of barley.

FRESH DATES – look at them carefully before you buy – the skins should be quite smooth with no wrinkles. Taste one if in doubt, for fresh dates may ferment if kept badly. You could substitute dried ones if necessary, but fresh ones are much better. Buy a handful per portion of the sweet.

BANANAS – buy them as ripe as possible, though not rotting. Count half of a biggish fruit per helping.

FUNGHI PORCINI – or dried ceps – buy from an Italian delicatessen; they are expensive in relation to their weight but be generous with them, especially as the barley is so cheap – allow 1 oz (25 g) for 4 portions or per pound (500 g) of barley.

BARLEY – tasty, nourishing, with a satisfying consistency and texture all of its own, yet surprisingly cheap. 1 lb (500 g) will serve 4.

DOUBLE CREAM – ½ pint (300 ml) will make 4 helpings of the sweet.

YOGHURT – to serve with the aubergine; real Greek yoghurt is what we like best; a 480 g (1 lb) carton will serve 4.

EGGS – 1 per aubergine.

OTHER INGREDIENTS – a handful or so of plain white flour to dust the aubergine fritters; a few tablespoons of olive oil to fry the aubergines and to cook the barley; a little parmesan if liked to serve with the barley.

WINE – white or red, even both, will go perfectly well with this simple meal of somewhat Eastern or Mediterranean character. Bulgaria is one of the world's biggest producers of wines – fifth at the last count – and well controlled, too, which makes choosing and buying cheap, straightforward and safe enough. Look for the name of the grape, avoiding wines with labels that don't give it, or which you cannot understand – go for muscat, riesling or chardonnay if you want white; cabernet, merlot, gamza or mavrud (the most Bulgarian of all) for red. We tried a 1981 merlot from the Haskovo region – a dark biggish wine you might well enjoy with the barley.

PREPARATION AND PRECOOKING

Make the sweet, the inspiration for which comes from Suzy Benghiat (*Middle Eastern Cookery*, Weidenfeld and Nicolson, 1984), 2-3 hours in advance.

Wash fresh but not dried dates under cold running water. With wet hands and a small sharp knife cut the ends off each date, slash the skin around the middle, and twist – one half against the other, making the skins come off whole more or less if the dates are really ripe. Halve them lengthwise, remove the stones, and lay the halves in a glass bowl until the bottom is covered.

Peel and slice the bananas, about ⅙ inch (4 mm) thick, as you go along – they will turn brown if you leave them uncovered too long.

Put a layer of banana slices on top of the dates already in the bowl, and cover with some of the double cream to prevent browning. Continue building up layers in this fashion until all the fruit is used up, then pour the remaining cream over the top to coat everything evenly and place in the refrigerator.

The barley and mushrooms, too, can be prepared in advance and reheated at the last minute.

Put the dried funghi porcini in a small bowl, cover but don't drown with tepid water and set aside to soak – this will take about 30 minutes.

Meanwhile peel and roughly chop the Spanish onion. Bring some water to the boil in the kettle, switch off, and keep it standing by. In a casserole heat a little olive oil over medium heat, soften the onion until it looks glassy, add the barley, cover with boiling water – about ½ inch (1 cm) deep – and simmer, checking the liquid level and stirring regularly. Add a little salt and pepper after 25 minutes.

Strain the soaked porcini through a sieve lined with a small piece of muslin, and add both the mushrooms and juice to the barley. Simmer for a further 10 minutes or so until the liquid has been absorbed and the barley is cooked. Test a few grains – they ought to be moist and soft, with some resistance to the bite and substance left. Cover and set aside, ready to reheat. Alternatively, stir in a knob of butter and serve.

Last, wash the aubergines; peel and chop the garlic and mix with the yoghurt; keep the yoghurt refrigerated until you serve it.

COOKING AND PRESENTATION

When your guests are sipping their first drinks, slice the aubergines lengthwise, about ½ inch (1 cm) thick. Distribute a little white flour on a flat surface and put down the slices, coating them slightly on both sides. In a mixing bowl, beat 1 egg for each aubergine. In a big frying pan or two if your party is big, heat some olive oil over medium heat. When the oil is hot, dip the flour-coated fritters into the egg and lay them in the pan side by side, without overlapping. Cook them until golden brown underneath – about 5 minutes – then turn and finish for not quite as long. Serve the fritters from the pan, with the yoghurt and garlic sauce on the side.

Reheat the barley and mushrooms; serve with grated parmesan on the side if you like, but be careful when sprinkling it over the top – Gerd at least thinks that parmesan is powerful enough to hide the rather more subtle flavour of the funghi.

Serve the date and banana dessert.

FLAT MEAT, ROUND DUMPLINGS

A short but varied menu, incorporating sweet
and sour, meat, vegetables, cheese and fruit.
It can all be prepared well in advance, leaving
you no more than a few minutes cooking at
the last moment.

Bresaola

Gnocchi verdi

Caramel oranges

*Grumello
Sforzato*

SHOPPING LIST

BRESAOLA – air-dried salt beef from the Lombard Valtellina,
which extends from Lake Como to the Stelvio Pass, under the
southern ramparts of the Swiss Alps. Bündnerfleisch is the
northern alternative to this delicacy which should be cut barely
more than paper-thin on a machine. Watch the slices peel off the
dark oblong block of meat and judge the quantity that way – 1
portion should cover a flat plate of good size, without overlaps.
Have them packed carefully, with layers of greaseproof paper in
between, and store in the refrigerator.

GNOCCHI VERDI – little spinach dumplings, light and easily
made. Here are the quantities for 6 helpings – 2 lb (1 kg) spinach;
4 eggs; 5 oz (150 g) butter; 1 lb (500 g) ricotta; 3 oz (75 g) grated

parmesan; 4 oz (125 g) plain white flour; a pinch of grated nutmeg; salt and fresh black pepper.

CARAMEL ORANGES – you might just find these already done in a shop, in which case take them provided they are moist and, literally, in good shape. Alternatively make them yourself, they're easy, and this is all you need – 1 orange, preferably of the tart Seville variety, per head; white granulated sugar – 8 oz (250 g) is plenty for 6; some cocktail sticks, 1 or 2 per orange.

LEMONS – to dress the bresaola; count a quarter of a ripe juicy fruit per starter.

OLIVE OIL – extra virgin, 1-2 tablespoons to dress 1 portion of bresaola.

BLACK PEPPER – each starter should be well covered with fresh ground pepper.

WINES – only the other day we asked at Lina's, our favourite Italian shop in Soho, where they bought their bresaola – from Montagna in Valtellina, was the reply, where Grumello is also made. Look for this fragrant red wine, made from the nebbiolo grape and grown on the mountainous south-facing slopes above the valley, it is one of four wines entitled to the DOC of Valtellina Superiore. Alternatively ask for the neighbouring Sassella, Inferno or Valgella. As for a pudding wine, red Sforzato, or Sfursat to give it its *romontsch* name, is the wine to try. Here are two wines we like, both from Casa Vinicola Nera – 1980 Grumello; 1980 Sforzato.

PREPARATION AND PRECOOKING

Make the caramel oranges well in advance, the night before if you like. In a small saucepan bring a little water to the boil. Meanwhile wash the oranges and dry. With a vegetable peeler, pare a little rind from each (say 2 or 3 strips), cut them into matchsticks, drop them into the boiling water for 3 minutes and drain, reserving the strips and liquid.

Peel the oranges with a sharp knife of medium size – first slice off the tops and bottoms, then set the oranges on a plate, and carefully cut down the sides, just deep enough to remove the white pith and transparent skins underneath; avoid undue pressure, and collect the juices on the plate; cut through the oranges horizontally into four or five slices each and reassemble, pinning the slices together again with one or two cocktail sticks each. Find a heatproof glass bowl to present the oranges in, arrange them side by side on the bottom and top with the strips of rind.

Pour the reserved orange liquid and juices into a measuring jug and top with water – for 8 oz (250 g) of granulated white sugar the total liquid should amount to 7½ fl oz (230 ml). Pour the liquid into a heavy saucepan and set it over the lowest possible heat. Weigh out the sugar and add, without stirring. Measure 2½ fl oz (70 ml) of warm water and set aside. When the sugar has dissolved, bring the mixture to the boil and cook steadily, on medium heat, until the mixture turns a rich brown. Shielding your hand with a cloth, quickly pour the warm water into the pan, stir until all lumps of caramel have dissolved and pour over the oranges in the bowl. Let them cool, then refrigerate.

Half a day in advance, if you like, pick over the spinach for the gnocchi, removing any long tough stems, and wash thoroughly in several changes of cold water. Put the dripping wet leaves in a saucepan, sprinkle with 1 teaspoon of salt for the quantities given in the shopping list, cover, and cook gently, stirring occasionally, until tender – after 10 minutes or so. Drain through a sieve, squeeze between layers of kitchen paper until quite dry, spread on a board and chop finely.

Break the eggs into a mixing bowl and beat with a fork or whisk until foaming.

In the same saucepan you used for the spinach, put 1 oz (25 g) of the butter, the ricotta, a pinch of grated nutmeg and the chopped spinach, together with a little salt and fresh pepper. Stir over very low heat until all the ingredients have mixed and appear quite dry, but be careful – the ricotta must not cook. Remove from the stove and beat in the grated parmesan, flour and eggs until all are thoroughly mixed. Set aside to cool, then put the mix in a bowl and refrigerate for at least 1 hour to firm up.

You can prepare the bresaola, too, well in advance, though an hour will do. Lay out each portion on a flat plate, with a minimum of overlap between slices. Cover them with extra virgin oil – 1-2 tablespoons per starter – sprinkle with the juice of a quarter lemon and plenty of fresh black pepper. Set aside in a cool place, ready to be served.

About half an hour before you wish to eat, prepare plenty of salty hot water to cook the gnocchi in – use a big saucepan, as for pasta, holding at least 1 gallon (4.5 litres).

COOKING AND PRESENTATION

Just before serving the first course, bring the water for the gnocchi to the boil, switch off, cover and keep standing by.

Take the gnocchi mix from the refrigerator. Sprinkle a board or similar surface with flour, and rub flour over your hands. With a teaspoon for a measure take some of the mix and roll it into a small ball, a little over 1 inch (2.5 cm) across; place the ball on the flour-covered board. Continue until all the mix is used up. Set the shaped dumplings aside in a cool place.

Serve the first course.

Return to the kitchen and bring the water back to the boil. Meanwhile find an ovenproof dish, put in 2 oz (50 g) of the butter, and put in the oven at gas 2/300°F/150°C. On a flat surface next to the cooker spread out a double layer of kitchen paper, big enough to drain the gnocchi on once they have been cooked.

When the water is boiling, reduce the heat to a slow simmer, carefully put in the first half of your gnocchi, and watch for them to return to the surface, 4-5 minutes. Lift them out with a perforated spoon and place on the kitchen paper.

Bring the water back to the boil, reduce to a simmer and put in the rest of the gnocchi. While they are cooking, carefully transfer the first load to the buttered bowl in the oven.

Let the second lot drain on kitchen paper for a moment or two, and put them, too, in the oven. Quickly melt the remaining 2 oz (50 g) of butter in a saucepan. When it is turning brown, take the gnocchi from the oven, pour the brown butter over, and serve immediately.

Offer the caramel oranges and Sforzato last.

ITALIAN, A BIT OF FRENCH AND PORTUGUESE TOO

A rustic menu you can easily adapt as regards numbers, and precook almost entirely. You will need two big frying pans, though, if you want to serve everything as crisp and freshly hot as possible.

Artichokes, with mustard dressing

Veal meatballs; polenta and tomato sauce

Goat cheeses

Fresh fruit

Sercial
Red wines from Portugal

SHOPPING LIST

ARTICHOKES – as for Menu 26 (see page 151), buy 1 globe per starter, well closed and round with a good strong stem.

LEMON – buy 1 to acidulate the water for the artichokes, and count an extra quarter lemon per head if you wish to offer finger bowls after the artichokes have been eaten.

FRUIT – it's unlikely appetites will remain unsatisfied at the end of this menu, but a little fresh fruit either to go with or round off the cheese is always welcome. The question is what you can find in winter, with local apples, pears and even nuts beyond their prime. New Granny Smiths from South America may be available, though – go for them if you can find them; alternatively choose something exotic like mangoes or guavas.

TOMATO SAUCE – for 6 portions of sauce you will need 1 small onion; 1 clove of garlic; 3 tablespoons olive oil; approximately 1 lb (500 g) creamed Italian tomatoes, either in a packet or in a can; 1 tablespoon tomato purée; 1 teaspoon dried mixed herbs; salt and pepper.

VEAL – 1 lb (500 g) of minced flank will serve 6, but be sure what you buy really is veal. If you can't be sure, ask for the cut first and only when you have seen it ask for it to be minced. Better still buy a good piece of a superior cut – silverside, for example – and mince it yourself by hand or with a food processor – if you have not tasted it before, the difference between that and butcher's mince may well surprise you.

OTHER INGREDIENTS FOR VEAL MEATBALLS – for 6 helpings you will need 2 oz (50 g) of white bread without crusts; a cup of milk to soak the bread; 3 cloves of garlic; 2 strips of lemon rind; 1 tablespoon of finely chopped parsley; 2 eggs; 1 oz (25 g) grated parmesan; a pinch of grated nutmeg; a handful or two of plain white flour to coat the meatballs; enough olive oil for shallow frying – i.e. ¼ inch (6 mm) deep in a sizable pan.

GOAT CHEESES – look for some little cheeses from different areas and of different ripenesses, if you like; for example – chabichou from Poitou, rocamadour from the Lot, buchette d'Anjou and brin d'Amour from Corsica; alternatively, or in addition, ask for what's new on the home front. Taste and buy by eye.

POLENTA – ground maize, usually available fine, medium and coarse; buy the coarsest you can find – 3 oz (75 g) per head.

MUSTARD DRESSING – 2 teaspoons of mustard, Dijon or similar, per artichoke; olive oil.

WINE – only a robust wine would go with an artichoke and mustard dressing, so desist or risk a lingering metallic flavour in your mouth, which may well spoil everything else to come. Take a glass of Sercial, dry Madeira, as an aperitif if you like, drink water or nothing with the starter, and change to Portugal proper with the main course. Prompted by WINE magazine, four of us tried three wines, of increasing age, with the same kind of food – 1982 Tinto da Anfora, João Pires; 1980 Camarate, Jose Maria de Fonseca; and 1977 Pasmados, also from Fonseca. The first was the strongest, with 13% alcohol, traditional in grapes and style and a year older than the one WINE had awarded three stars to; Camarate was a more modern wine, containing also cabernet and merlot, or so we had read; while the oldest, Pasmados, was traditional again. Our winner? The first, by a narrow margin. But half a bottle of the Pasmados was left over at the end, and two of us tried that again the next day – it could well have been the winner had it opened up as much during dinner, deep and soft, with a long pleasant aftertaste. So, try and come to your own conclusions – it seems Portugal is well on the way from those huge Dãos we remember without much pleasure.

PREPARATION AND PRECOOKING

Several hours in advance, even in the morning if cooking for dinner, set enough well salted water to boil in a big stainless steel saucepan that will not discolour the artichokes, lid on.

Meanwhile wash the artichokes in plenty of cold water, making sure nothing is trapped between the leaves, especially if there are gaps. Trim the stems back to the base of the globes but don't throw them away – the top end is perfectly edible if stringed, which you can do after cooking.

Squeeze a lemon and set aside the juice.

When the water is boiling fast, pour in the lemon juice, wait for the froth to disappear and put in the artichokes. Let the water come back to the boil for a minute or two, then simmer, lid on. Set the timer for 20 minutes.

Get the water for the polenta going – allow about ½ pint (300 ml) for each 3 oz (75 g) portion. Salt the water lightly and cover; weigh out the polenta and set aside.

Add the artichoke stalks to the pan about 10 minutes before the globes are ready. When the time is up, test by pulling off an outer leaf – the thick end should be soft when done, but not soggy. Drain through a colander, turn the artichokes upside down and let drip, together with the stalks.

When the polenta water is boiling, pour in the polenta, stir and reduce the heat to a simmer, lid half on. Watch the polenta thicken almost immediately. Stir frequently to prevent sticking for 20-25 minutes, when all the water will have disappeared. Turn the polenta out on to a clean flat surface or platter and spread with a spatula or knife about 1 inch (2.5 cm) thick. Leave to cool.

Prepare the tomato sauce next, ingredients as given in the shopping list or in proportion. Peel and finely chop the onion and clove of garlic. In a frying pan warm 2 tablespoons of olive oil, add the chopped onion and garlic and cook gently, making sure the garlic does not burn. Add the creamed Italian tomatoes, tomato purée, dried mixed herbs and a little salt, and simmer for 15 minutes.

Unless the veal is minced already, mince it now, using a food processor or a heavy knife which must be very sharp or you will squash the meat rather than cut it, losing its juices as you work – this is the objection to mincers, which, once they have finished, tend to leave tasteless dry meat fibres mixed with fat alone. With a small knife first remove all fat, gristle and other connective tissue from the meat; cut it into small pieces and process, or continue chopping with a rhythmical rocking motion of the blade, working from side to side and back again, until you have a smooth moist paste.

Take the tomato sauce from the heat and work it through a sieve. Prepare the other ingredients for the meatballs, quantities as given in the shopping list or in proportion. Break the bread into small pieces and put into a mixing bowl. Scarcely cover with milk and leave for 10 minutes to soften.

Meanwhile peel and crush the garlic. Pare 2 thin strips of rind from a lemon and chop finely, together with the fresh parsley. Break the eggs into a large bowl and beat with a fork or whisk.

Strain and discard excess liquid from the bread and milk in the mixing bowl. Add the minced veal, garlic, lemon rind, parsley and eggs. Add the grated parmesan, a pinch of grated nutmeg, salt and fresh black pepper, and mix well.

You can stop your preparations here provided you refrigerate the meatball mixture and keep the polenta in one slab in a cool place, covered loosely; the tomato sauce and artichokes, too, should be kept cool.

About 20 minutes before dinner take the meatball mix from the refrigerator. Make the mustard dressing for the artichokes – in a small jug or mixing bowl, for each artichoke put 2 teaspoons of mustard and whisk in drop by drop some olive oil, until you have a thick sauce of even consistency; set the sauce aside in a cool place ready for serving.

Prepare two big frying pans – one for the polenta, the other for the meatballs.

COOKING AND PRESENTATION

While your guests are enjoying their first drink, quickly warm about ⅛ inch (3 mm) olive oil in the first frying pan, cut the polenta into portions, and begin to cook it gently over low heat, for 15 minutes on the first side.

Meanwhile shape the meatballs. Flour your hands. Flour a board or similar working surface. With a teaspoon take the meatball mix from the bowl and form into round balls – a little over 1 inch (2.5 cm) across. Place them on the floured board as you continue, until all the mix is used up and they are all thinly but evenly coated with flour.

With the polenta fried and crisp on one side only, take it from the heat and join your guests for the first course. Serve the artichokes with the mustard dressing on the side. Put a big plate or platter on the table for debris leaves, and lay knives and forks to cut the chokes from the bottoms. Offer finger bowls if you like – small bowls of warm water and quarter chunks of lemon – or extra napkins.

Return to the kitchen and begin frying the polenta on the second side. Put the tomato sauce in a pan and heat gently.

In the second frying pan heat about ¼ inch (6 mm) of olive oil and put in the meatballs – in batches if necessary – frying them for 3 minutes on one side, then another 3 on the opposite side. Keep the first batch hot in the tomato sauce. Then serve quickly, portioning everything out straight from the pans.

Serve the cheeses and fruit last.

STARTING LIGHTLY

A menu you can prepare well in advance or even buy ready-made if you want to save the time it takes to prepare the first course and the potato salad. You will need nothing special in terms of equipment, just make sure you have some foil for the papillote – one or more – to cook the pork in.

Mushrooms à la grecque

Fillet of pork en papillote; potato salad

Tiramisu

Australian wines

SHOPPING LIST

MUSHROOMS À LA GRECQUE – not nearly as Greek as the French term suggests, applying to all sorts of vegetables cooked in olive oil and served at room temperature. They are available ready to take away in many good delicatessens – buy by eye provided you like the look and scent of what you see on offer, or make them yourself – few starters are prepared more easily than this one. Here are the ingredients and approximate quantities for 4 helpings of our somewhat unorthodox recipe – 8 oz (250 g) button mushrooms, small enough to leave whole; 1 shallot or small onion; 2 cloves of garlic; 2-3 tomatoes; 4 tablespoons extra virgin oil; 1 tablespoon tomato purée; 10 peppercorns; ½ tablespoon dried mixed herbs; 1 tablespoon good red wine; 1 teaspoon lemon juice; a little salt.

LEEKS – get 4 small or 2 bigger leeks, approximately similar in size, to go with each fillet of pork.

POTATOES – you can find potato salad ready-made; if you prefer to make it yourself buy small new potatoes, a handful per helping.

PORK FILLET – order this cut well in advance, as it is not always available. One whole fillet, weighing just over 12 oz (350 g) serves 2.

TIRAMISU – means pick-me-up in Italian, perhaps because of the sheer energy contained in this Marsala-laced pudding. Here are the ingredients for 8 or more – about ½ pint (300 ml) very strong black coffee, as strong as espresso if possible; 5 eggs; 2 table-spoons of caster sugar; 1 lb (500 g) mascarpone (Italian cream cheese with a consistency similar to that of clotted cream); ⅓ cup of Marsala, a dessert wine from Sicily – but beware of so-called cooking Marsala, or, worse still, one of those concoctions mixed with eggs already in bottle – use a good sherry, Madeira or even port if you can't lay your hands on the real article, such as produced by Marco de Bartoli, for example; a small packet of sponge fingers; 2 oz (50 g) bitter chocolate, grated.

OTHER INGREDIENTS – olive oil, mustard, white wine vinegar, salt and pepper to dress the potato salad if making; olive oil for brushing the fillets; white bread to serve with the mushrooms à la grecque.

WINES – There are now interesting new young white wines reaching our markets from Austria and New Zealand, and so we tried one, followed by an older red, both from the Old Triangle Vineyard, Hill-Smith Estate, Barossa Valley, South Australia – first a 1986 Young Style Rhine Riesling, green almost, and dry, with a delicate scent of grapes, and a rather more mature though far from heavy 1984 Shiraz-Malbec, made from a mix of black grapes we would normally associate with Rhone (Shiraz) and Bordeaux (Malbec). We liked them, and they went well with this menu, which otherwise might be an ideal candidate for a gewürztraminer, especially with the pork.

PREPARATION AND PRECOOKING

Make the tiramisu the night before – quantities as given in the shopping list or in proportion.

First, make the required quantity of coffee – as strong as you can, but not with instant, please – and let it cool.

Meanwhile separate the eggs. Put the yolks in a sizable mixing bowl, beat in the sugar, then mix in the mascarpone. In a second bowl beat the whites with a rotary or wire whisk until quite stiff, and fold loosely into the mascarpone mix.

Find a glass bowl or similar with straight sides and a wide flat bottom in which to make and present the pudding. Mix the coffee and Marsala together. Just for a moment dunk a sponge finger into the coffee-Marsala mix, then lay it on the bottom of the bowl. Repeat until the bottom is covered with a neat single layer. Put half of the mascarpone mix on top and level it out carefully. Put another layer of sponge fingers dunked in coffee and Marsala on top, and cover that with the rest of the mascarpone mix. Once again level out the layer, and sprinkle the grated chocolate over the top. Put the completed tiramisu in the refrigerator for at least 3 hours.

Unless you decide to buy them ready-made, you can prepare the mushrooms in advance, too – again, quantities as given in the shopping list or pro rata.

Peel and finely chop the shallot and garlic cloves. Put the tomatoes in a mixing bowl and scald with boiling water from the kettle. Peel and cut them in half, scoop out seeds, and chop roughly.

In a heavy saucepan warm the olive oil, put in the chopped shallot and garlic, and cook gently for a few minutes, taking care not to burn the garlic.

Meanwhile wash the mushrooms and dry, being careful not to let them absorb any water – if they do, they will expel it again when cooking, thus diluting the flavour. With a sharp knife, trim the stems and cut away loose or ragged edges.

When the shallot is soft, add the chopped tomatoes, tomato purée, whole button mushrooms, peppercorns, herbs, wine and a little salt, and simmer for about 10 minutes, lid on. Stir occasionally to prevent sticking. Off the heat, add the lemon juice, stir, transfer into a serving bowl, and set aside to cool – don't refrigerate mushrooms à la grecque, as they are meant to be eaten at room temperature.

Unless you decide to buy the potato salad ready-made, prepare it in the morning if you like, but at least an hour in advance, when you should also take the fillet of pork from the refrigerator to let it warm to room temperature.

First, choose a saucepan big enough to boil the potatoes in, put in sufficient water to cover, salt, and boil on high heat, lid on.

Meanwhile wash and scrub the potatoes under running cold water, but leave the skins intact.

When the water is boiling fast, drop in the potatoes, let the water come back to the boil and reduce the heat a little, so that the water is still lively but not fierce. Test after 12 minutes.

Meanwhile, make a dressing of mustard, olive oil, a little wine vinegar, salt and fresh black pepper. When the potatoes are done, drain them through a colander, let dry for a minute or two, then chop them into slices about ¼ inch (6 mm) thick with a sharp knife. Put them in a bowl, cover with the dressing, toss gently and set aside to cool. Toss every now and then and serve tepid or cold.

Finally, prepare the leeks and pork for the oven. Rinse, top and tail the leeks first. Leave them whole if small, slice them length-wise in half if bigger, but in any case check no earth is trapped between the leaves. On a flat surface, measure out a piece of foil big enough to make an envelope for each fillet.

Brush the foil with olive oil, put down 2 leeks or leek halves and pour a little oil over them; rub the fillet with salt and pepper then oil and place on top of the leeks; put the remaining 2 leeks or leek halves on top of the meat, oil and sprinkle with a little more salt and plenty of black pepper. You don't want super-hot steam drying out the meat inside the papillote, so seal the foil quite tightly around its contents, making an airtight parcel with triple folds at the seam.

Assuming your guests will be reasonably punctual, put the papillote or papillotes in the oven about 10 minutes before they are due, and switch to gas 2/300°F/150°C – the meat and leeks will be ready to eat in 35-40 minutes.

COOKING AND PRESENTATION

Serve the mushrooms à la grecque with a little white bread on the side.

Return to the kitchen, take the papillotes from the oven when done, and open carefully in order not to lose the cooking juices inside. Carve each fillet with a sharp knife into diagonal slices about ¼ inch (6 mm) thick, and portion out on to individual plates – half a fillet plus 2 small leeks or equivalent per portion, with a tablespoon or so of the cooking juices on top. Offer the potato salad on the side.

Last offer the tiramisu, straight from the chilled bowl.

SAUSAGE AND BEANS

A sturdy repast, southern peasant in style, which you can prepare quickly and well in advance – as much as three days in advance for the dried fruit salad – and stretch easily, for as many guests as you like.

Tapenade

Cotechino and butter beans

Dried fruit salad

1981 Marques de Murrieta, Rioja white
1980 Regaleali Rosso del Conte
Bukkuram, Moscato Passito di Pantelleria,
Marco de Bartoli

SHOPPING LIST

TAPENADE – for 4 helpings you will need 2 dozen black olives; 8 anchovy fillets; 2 tablespoons of capers; 2 oz (50 g) canned tuna; 3-4 tablespoons of extra virgin olive oil, depending on the thickness of sauce you want to achieve; about 1 tablespoon lemon juice, according to taste; black pepper.

EGGS – to serve with the tapenade; count 1 whole hard-boiled egg per head.

COTECHINO – a speciality of the central Italian province of Emilia originally, made also in neighbouring Modena, where most of these fresh pork sausages come from nowadays. *Cotica*, pork rind, is the essential ingredient, and it alone should be ground in a fine cotechino, whereas the meat and spices are pounded in a mortar. There is certainly a difference between the traditional recipe and poorer industrial varieties, so ask for advice in a good Italian shop, and buy it cooked rather than uncooked, with an eye on the maker's date stamp. 1 whole sausage may be enough to feed 4, but sizes vary, as do appetites – look at the sausage and imagine it cut in portions. Store it in your refrigerator, where it should keep for a few days. If you cannot find a precooked cotechino, consider cooking it yourself – all you need do is simmer it gently in water for about 2 hours.

VEGETABLES AND HERBS – to cook with the beans. You will need, per pound (500 g) of beans, 4 medium shallots; 2 cloves of garlic; 3 celery stalks; 2 medium leeks; a handful of parsley; a few sprigs of thyme; 1 bay leaf.

DRIED FRUIT – the choice is great and yours, but here are the ingredients Suzy Benghiat (*Middle Eastern Cookery*, Weidenfeld and Nicholson, 1984) lists for a big khochaf, a dried fruit salad, that improves for several days in the refrigerator – 4 oz (125 g) each of raisins, sultanas, dried peaches and apricots, plus double that of dried prunes, and an optional piece of amardine (apricot paste), about 4 inches (10 cm) square. In addition, she suggests, you might serve a few roasted almonds, or other nuts, with each helping, plus a little rose or orange water to freshen the mix. We have found that the juice of 1 lemon also improves the flavour of this dish, which, as given here, easily yields 12 helpings if not more. Where to get all these things? Dried fruit and nuts – in a health food store; amardine – in a mid-eastern food store, which you may be able to trace through your *Yellow Pages*; rose and orange water – from a good chemist.

DRIED BEANS – with their satisfying big shapes, good butter beans from a recent harvest are always fun, but smaller cannellini or borlotti beans make excellent alternatives. Ask which kind is freshest if in doubt, and inspect butter beans especially – avoid them if they look dull and broken. About 1 lb (500 g) will make 4 generous portions.

BOTTLED WATER – the dried fruit will have to soak in water for at least 3 days – long enough for chlorinated tap water to leave its unpleasant traces. Unless you live in the country and are lucky enough to have good running water, get a big 2-litre bottle of still table water to start with, and have some more standing by to top up as necessary.

OTHER INGREDIENTS – a little fresh white bread would go well with the tapenade; some mustard, a good Dijon or moutarde de Meaux, to serve with the beans.

WINES – a tapenade with hard-boiled eggs is a tough proposition for any wine, white or red, and too much for most – that's why we tried the Marques de Murrieta's old-style white Rioja of 1981, intense and with a strong aroma of oak we rather like. Of course, if you start with big flavours it would be unwise to drink down, and hence the rest of the list is strong – the Rosso del Conte is Sicily's finest red, with great strength and rather more serious qualities than our modest peasant dish perhaps deserves; but they go together surprisingly well and lead on perfectly to a stronger wine yet, one geographically suited to the mid-eastern pudding. Bukkuram, so the numbered label on the back of the bottle explained, is the father of the vine, and the wine itself is made by the classic method of vinification that the Arabs introduced to this almost African island only God knows when. It's a naturally sweet wine, rich and grapey, one to sit with in gentle conversation or wondering quietly how it came about that we may enjoy the extraordinary complex and living flavours we call wine.

PREPARATION AND PRECOOKING

Make the dried fruit salad 3 or even 4 days in advance. With a sharp knife cut larger fruit into pieces, but leave prunes and anything smaller intact. If you have some amardine cut it into small squares with wet kitchen scissors – about ½ inch (1 cm) big – and add to the mix. Find the biggest bowl you can fit into your refrigerator, for the fruit will swell considerably as their liquid levels are restored; put in all the dried fruit, together with the juice of 1 lemon, cover with 2 inches (5 cm) of bottled water, stir and put in the refrigerator for 3 days. Keep stirring every now and then, and watch the liquid level – the fruit should remain covered at all times.

Soak the beans in cold water the night before, or cover with boiling water and let stand for 2-3 hours, when they should be ready to cook.

Precook the cotechino if necessary – in a heavy saucepan cover it well with water and simmer gently for 2 hours; don't pierce the skin as some recipes suggest or you will lose much of the flavour.

Prepare the beans and cotechino in the morning if you like – all quantities as given in the shopping list or pro rata. First peel and finely chop the shallots and garlic. In a heavy casserole warm 4 tablespoons of olive oil. Add the shallots and cook gently until soft. Meanwhile fill the kettle and bring to the boil. Quickly pull away strings from the celery, and check no earth is hiding in the green roll of leek leaves, then wash, dry and chop with the parsley and thyme. Put the beans, chopped garlic, vegetables and all the herbs but no salt in the casserole; just cover with boiling water, boil for 10 minutes then simmer, lid on, for 20 minutes.

With a sharp knife cut the cotechino into slices 1 inch (2.5 cm) thick and add to the beans together with a teaspoon of salt, making sure the sausage is well covered with liquid. Replace the lid and continue to simmer for 25 minutes more or so, until the beans are soft but with some resistance to the bite left. Unless you are ready to serve the dish now, replace the lid and set aside to cool.

Prepare the tapenade and hard-boiled eggs last, an hour or so before the meal. Carefully put the eggs into a saucepan, cover well with cold water and bring to the boil slowly. Reduce to a simmer and set the timer for 10 minutes.

Meanwhile make the tapenade – quantities as in the shopping list or in proportion. Stone the olives and put in a mortar. Add the anchovy fillets, capers, tuna and a few drops of olive oil. Pound until you get a rough paste. Continue pounding, adding a little more olive oil as for a mayonnaise – i.e. in small quantities, no faster than you can work it into the sauce. When the sauce is smooth and shiny, add a little lemon juice and fresh black pepper, and set aside, ready to serve.

When the time for the eggs is up, quickly but carefully plunge them into cold, not tepid, water, leave them for a minute or two, then set aside to dry.

PRESENTATION

Gently reheat the cotechino and beans while you serve and eat the first course.

Offer the hard-boiled eggs in a basket, still in their shells, with the tapenade and some white bread on the side. Let each guest do his or her own thing – for example, you can cut the shelled egg in half, scoop out the yolk, mix it with the tapenade and replace in the empty white.

Serve the beans and cotechino in big soup plates, with knives, forks and spoons, too. Offer mustard on the side – a good Dijon or moutarde de Meaux, for example.

Offer the dried fruit salad in small bowls, filled straight from the big bowl in the refrigerator, with a glass or two of the Bukkuram on the side.

POUR CELEBRER LE BEAUJOLAIS NOUVEAU

Mouth-watering and a pleasure to choose,
buy and carry home as much as to eat, or so
we imagine this spread, with a bottle of lively
new *beaujolly* per head to drive out cold and
gloom . . .

*An abundance of pies, ballotines, terrines,
galantines, rillettes and sausages from the
charcuterie counter, accompanied by pickles, fresh
hard butter and home-baked wholemeal bread,
crudités and a hearty salad of Batavian endive and
oak leaves, with a spicy tarragon vinegar dressing*

*Camembert, pont-l'eveque and other Normandy
cheeses*

*Beaujolais nouveau, of course
1982 Châteauneuf du Pape, Chante Cigale*

SHOPPING LIST

CHARCUTERIE – first locate your source or sources, British and
foreign in terms of produce, then pounce and carry off what is
freshest and best, buying entirely by eye and taste if you can.
Make a list first of the various types of cured and cooked meats,
sausages, pies and pâtés you fancy, then try to buy a little of
each, avoiding overlap of those too alike. Here, for example, is a
selection we might look for – cooked York ham; smoked ham

from Westphalia; salt-cured prosciutto crudo; chunks of mortadella and coarse salame casalinga; paper-thin slices of a hard Hungarian salame; big wheels of Bavarian Zungenwurst and little South Tirolean Kamminwurzen; spicy smoked sausages; a selection of English game pies, whole if small, or slices if big; pork, goose and duck rillettes from France; salt beef, cooked tongue and Bündnerfleisch or bresaola dressed with oil and lemon; brawn and fresh black pudding . . .

CHEESES – a white round camembert and a whole golden square of pont-l'eveque of comparable size, plus an orange livarot, round again and aged in special rooms where no fresh air must enter – three flavours not unrelated but holding their own, listed here in rising order of strength. Be careful, though, when buying whole cheeses you cannot taste until you cut them at home – first of all try to buy them from a place with a good turnover and someone willing to tell you what to look for or what to avoid – such as a scent of ammonia or shapes that don't fill their boxes any longer. Camembert and pont-l'eveque are each exported in a small container with paper wrapping sticking to oozing rinds. However, in winter all of these cheeses ought to be at their best, and so transport and keeping should pose no problems; don't be discouraged – look around a bit and you will find what you want.

SALAD – a little endive and oak, green and red, would go well with a feast of this kind, but be guided by quality first, for winter can be a hard time for leaf salads of substance. Go for relatively safe chicory and buttery little fennel bulbs if in doubt. Buy enough to make a big bowl of salad, inviting everyone to tuck in.

PICKLES – sweet and sour gherkins; big salt gherkins; sweet green, red and yellow peppers; dried tomatoes, funghi porcini and artichoke hearts preserved in olive oil; small pickled onions; walnuts; corn on the cob – the choice is not endless, but nearly so. In addition consider a choice of mustards – English, Dijon, Meaux . . .

TARRAGON VINEGAR DRESSING – this vinegar is easily found, with a spicy flavour especially suitable in conjunction with cold meats and mustard; mix it with a good olive oil, even walnut oil for the dressing if you like.

BREAD – you can buy it of course, but we would make our own for a feast of the kind. For 12 wholemeal rolls buy 7 oz (200 g) each of Granary malted brown and any other good wholemeal flour; 1 oz (25 g) each of whole wheat grains, rye grains, lard and fresh yeast; 1 teaspoon of salt.

BEAUJOLAIS NOUVEAU – November 16 usually brings the release of this modern marketing success we are beginning to take for granted, and which nowadays uses up at least half the crop of the local gamay grapes each year. Years and vintages vary, of course, as do styles of this almost violet wine with the scent of boiled sweets and very limited ageing potential – whole bunches of grapes are subjected to a process called carbonic maceration rather than the traditional presses, which makes for light fruity wines without the tannin necessary to let them last. So, strictly in winter, while it lasts, why not try more than one, perhaps in the form of a fun blind tasting? Here are the names of some shippers whose beaujolais nouveaux we have enjoyed over the last few years – Joseph Drouhin, Georges Duboeuf, Pasquier Desvignes, Loron, Sarrau; we also made cardinals for aperitifs when we felt we wanted a change – a thimble of cassis per glass does the trick.

CHÂTEAUNEUF DU PAPE – friends brought back a bottle of 1982 Chante Cigale for us, and we drank it, perhaps a little sooner than we ought to have done. However, it is considered 'drinking now' in the trade, we liked it and believe it would bring a welcome change after all that beaujolais – deeper, more solid and warm, promising another summer and vintage to come.

PREPARATION AND PRECOOKING

Make the bread first. This recipe takes about 2 ½ hours from start to finish, but only 5 minutes of actual work. It also calls for a little more yeast than is usual, which makes things very easy indeed, provided you don't kill the yeast by using hot water on it. You can experiment with all sorts of grains and flour. You will need a processor, though, with a plastic blade – a steel one would cut everything, grains included, into tiny pieces.

Bread quantities as given in the shopping list, or in proportion. Put the flour, grains, salt and lard into the processor. Process until mixed, then switch off.

Dissolve the yeast in ½ pint (300 ml) tepid – never hot – water, and stir until dissolved.

Turn on the processor again, add the liquid yeast from the top, and watch for the dough to form – 1-2 minutes, and you should have a ball. If it looks very sticky, add 1 tablespoon of strong white flour through the top of the machine. Turn the dough out into a large bowl, cover with a plastic bag and leave to rise for 1 hour in a warm place.

When the dough has risen and approximately doubled in size, grease a large baking tray. Flour your hands and shape the dough into rolls – a small handful for each will be about right – and place on the tray in rows, not too close together. Leave for 30 minutes until the rolls rise again.

Meanwhile preheat the oven to gas 8/450°F/230°C. Put in the rolls and bake for 20 minutes. Remove the tray and carefully prise the rolls from it with a palette knife or kitchen slice and set to cool on a wire rack – they will end up soggy if you leave them on the tray or place them on a solid surface.

You can freeze home-made rolls as soon as they have cooled, with minimum loss of freshness. To defrost simply put them, direct from the freezer, in a cold oven; turn to gas 4/350°F/180°C, and leave there for 15 minutes.

Beaujolais nouveau is always drunk cool, even iced by some, though we don't recommend that. An hour before dinner put the bottles in a cold room or outside, or in the refrigerator if necessary.

Prepare the salad next. Whatever you have bought, discard the outer leaves and inspect the inner ones. Wash if necessary and dry them in a salad centrifuge or by swinging them vigorously in a clean cloth or plastic basket. Trim, break them by hand and put in a big bowl, which you might also put in a cold room for the time being. Do not dress the salad yet.

If the cheeses are in the refrigerator or a very cold room, bring them in and let them warm just slightly – less than to room temperature if the central heating is at full blast.

Lay out the various kinds of charcuterie on platters, plates and boards. Put the pickles in bowls, and group the mustard pots on plates with separate spoons.

PRESENTATION

Put everything except the cheeses on a big table, preferably in a room different from the one where you are having your cardinals or first glasses of nouveau. Otherwise bring the food in a little later, or risk losing half before the start.

Toss the salad at the last moment. Make a strong dressing – about 1 tablespoon of tarragon vinegar to 4 of olive or walnut oil, a little salt, plenty of black pepper – and toss vigorously, preferably with your hands, until everything is evenly coated.

Serve the cheeses last, after a suitable break, and change the wine.

TO SEE OUT WINTER

If you like pancakes, here is a menu for
Shrove Tuesday which leaves enough room
for them at the end, and, altogether, requires
little preparation and only minimal cooking.
You'll need a sizable, preferably iron, frying
pan for the pancakes, and a small piece of
muslin to strain the burghul that goes into the
tabbouleh.

Tabbouleh

Scallops and prawns, sautéed in butter

Pancakes, with marmalade, jam and lemon filling

Blanquette de Limoux
Tokay Aszu, 3 puttonyos

SHOPPING LIST

TABBOULEH – one of the coolest and most appetizing dishes we
know. It is suitable as a starter as well as a little salad in between,
and is made very simply, with no cooking, in 20 minutes or so.
For 4-5 helpings you will need 6 tablespoons burghul, a kind of
precooked cracked wheat; 1 medium cucumber; 2 tomatoes; 8
spring onions; 2 handfuls of parsley, which ought to produce 2
cups of it finely chopped; 2 tablespoons chopped fresh mint;
juice of 1 lemon; 4 tablespoons olive oil; salt.

PARSLEY – get some extra, in addition to what you need for the tabbouleh – a tablespoon when chopped per portion or so.

GARLIC – a few cloves will do, say 1 clove per 2 or even 3 portions.

SCALLOPS – these don't crawl on the sea bed as other molluscs do, but propel themselves by opening and closing their shells with a powerful muscle, which is the main part we eat. Buy them fresh, and have them cleaned so that you get the white cylindrical muscle and the orange half moon of roe from each – count 3 per head.

PRAWNS – fresh and uncooked in their shells, counting 10 per head.

PANCAKES – for a basic light mix, enough to make 8-10 pancakes, you will need 4 oz (125 g) plain white flour; 1 egg; ½ pint (300 ml) milk; a pinch of salt. You can add a second egg and a tablespoon of melted butter too, if you like a richer batter – it's up to you and how hungry you think you will be at the end of this meal.

MARMALADE, JAMS, LEMONS – a choice of apricot and black cherry jams would go well with a really fine marmalade or simple lemon filling, or lemon juice and sugar for the lightest filling of all.

OTHER INGREDIENTS – vegetable oil for frying; white bread for serving with the scallops, if liked.

BLANQUETTE DE LIMOUX – a sparkling white wine from Languedoc, which we discovered but a few months ago – fresh, dry, with a light but distinct scent of fruit. Made by the méthode champenoise from the local mauzac grape and blended with a little chardonnay, it enjoys an appellation all of its own, and rightly so – Hugh Johnson judges it the best sparkling wine of the south of France, explaining its quality by the altitude of the hills where it is grown and the cool Atlantic breezes that temper the southern sun there.

Tokay – Aszu is the sweet variety of this famous, not quite sherry-like, wine made from the furmint and harslevelu grapes with the help of botrytis or noble rot. It is available in 3, 4 and 5 puttonyos quality (puttonyos meaning tub); the more 30-litre tubs of botrytis-affected grapes that are blended in, the more select and sweet the wine. Hungary is famous for its pancakes – *palacsinta* – too, and this led us to to try and suggest this wine; a wine showing 3 puttonyos has enough acidity left to go with a sweet dish.

PREPARATION AND PRECOOKING

Make the tabbouleh in the morning, if you like, but long enough in advance to chill – quantities as given in the shopping list or in proportion. First, put the burghul into a big bowl, top with plenty of cold water and leave to soak for 15 minutes.

Meanwhile peel the cucumber, cut in half lengthways, deseed with a teaspoon, cut into long strips about ¼ inch (6 mm) thick and then chop across to make dice of that size. Put the dice into a colander, sprinkle with salt, and squeeze for 2-3 minutes until a good deal of liquid has gone and the dice take on a glassy look and consistency.

Bring some water to boil in the kettle, scald the tomatoes, peel, cut in half, deseed with a teaspoon and chop finely.

With a sharp knife finely chop the spring onions, parsley and mint. Squeeze the juice from the lemon.

When the 15 minutes are up, line a sieve or colander with a piece of muslin, strain the soaked burghul through it, lift it out in the cloth and squeeze to remove all the surplus water.

Turn the burghul into a bowl and mix with all the ingredients you have prepared, plus 4 tablespoons of olive oil – extra virgin if possible – a little salt and fresh black pepper. Cover and put in the refrigerator until serving.

An hour before the appointed time, make sure the sparkling wine is getting cold, and prepare the batter for the pancakes – quantities as given in the shopping list or pro rata.

Weigh out the flour, and quickly work it through a sieve into a biggish mixing bowl. Make a shallow hole in the middle, break in the egg, and mix until you get a smooth paste. Add a pinch of salt and a few drops of milk, and stir or whisk until the milk has all been absorbed without lumps; gradually increase the flow until all the milk is used up and you have a mix of a consistency similar to that of single cream. Don't worry if you find lumps after all – simply work the batter through a fine sieve into another bowl. Put it in a cool place or the refrigerator to stand.

Check your pan for the pancakes. If it's an iron pan – has it been used recently? Or is it a little rusty? Clean it with a fine abrasive if necessary, but make sure you rinse it well under running hot water for some time. Dry it carefully, then prime the pan or it will not work later – put it on low heat, fill it with oil – any vegetable oil will do – about ¼ inch (6 mm) deep and let it heat until the oil shows signs of smoking. Remove from the heat, let the oil cool and pour it away – the pan is now primed, and should be cleaned with kitchen paper or a cloth only.

Chop the parsley and garlic for the main course.

Last, take the prawns from the refrigerator and shell – holding the tail with one hand and head with the other, straighten them out, gently push them together and twist, pulling off the tail shell in one piece. Discard the heads and return the prepared shelled tails to the refrigerator – they are thin enough not to need much warming before you cook them. Rinse your hands under cold water – warmth opens the pores – and wipe with a slice of lemon to get rid of the smell.

COOKING AND PRESENTATION

Take the scallops and prawns from the refrigerator about half an hour before you cook them.

Serve the tabbouleh first, on its own or with the main course if you prefer.

In a heavy frying pan melt a good knob of butter, put in the chopped garlic and cook gently, making sure the garlic does not burn. Put in the white muscle part of the scallops alone for 1 minute and turn for another, then add the prawns, and the orange scallop roes last. Add the parsley, a little salt and black pepper, and cook for approximately 5 minutes in all. Serve straight from the pan, with a little white bread on the side if you like.

Make the pancakes and serve them from the pan – hard on the cook unless there are two of you, but the only way to enjoy them at their best.

Put the lemon juice, sugar, marmalade and jams on the table, arranged in small jugs and bowls; alternatively place the various jars on a platter or big plate, and serve with an array of pretty spoons.

Take the batter from the refrigerator and stir until everything appears perfectly smooth.

Wipe the primed pan with a piece of kitchen paper saturated with oil – groundnut or corn, or even olive if you don't mind the slight taste it will impart.

Over medium, not quite high, heat, let the pan get hot until you see a haze rising over the surface. Ladle in enough batter to cover the bottom thinly – this may take one or two tries to get right, but the first couple of pancakes from a newly primed pan won't be at their best anyway, so don't worry about waste. With a spatula run round the rim of the flat bottom and watch it lift slightly. Turn the pancake with the spatula – or toss it if you have the knack – cook for a little longer and serve with the Tokay at room temperature or slightly below.

INDEX